The Sea Angler's First Handbook

Arthur E. Hardy was born in London and now lives in Bishop's Stortford. He started fishing when he was six years old and now applies the wide knowledge gained from almost forty years of angling all over the British Isles and Southern Ireland. His articles and stories have appeared in *Fishing Gazette* and *Angling Magazine*.

Alan Vare, who contributes the notes on tackle, has been a fishing tackle retailer for thirteen years and is currently lecturing on fishing, casting and fly-fishing at the East Herts College of Further Education. He has fished all over the world for almost thirty years.

Also in the Pan Anglers' Library

Pan Anglers' Library

The Sea Angler's First Handbook

Alan Vare and
Arthur E. Hardy

Pan Books London and Sydney

First published 1975 by Pelham Books Ltd
This edition published 1980 by Pan Books Ltd
Cavaye Place, London SW10 9PG
© Alan Vare and Arthur E. Hardy
ISBN 0 330 25991 1
Made and printed in Great Britain by
C. Nicholls & Company Ltd, Philips Park Press, Manchester

Contents

Illustrations

Figures

line drawings by Ted Andrews and Alan Vare

Introduction

Wherever you live in Britain, you're unlikely to be more than about sixty miles from the coast, with the choice of mile upon mile of shoreline, ranging from the stormy windswept waters of the north and east, to the sandy, sheltered coasts of the south and south-west, and, with a little research and experience, every mile will offer a wide variety of sportfishing.

Furthermore, this sea angling is a sport with an added bonus – fresh fish for the table, which can be pure delight in these days of deep-frozen pre-packaged living.

Of the three main types of angling, sea fishing is, without doubt, the most varied and challenging, particularly with regard to the different species that can be caught, and the almost never-ending variety of places to be discovered and explored. Sand, rock, shingle or wreck will all yield their particular varieties of fish, and, just when the angler thinks he really knows a piece of water, so he gets an unexpected surprise – usually in the form of a species of fish he has never caught before and which, in all probability, could be a rare visitor to that area.

Imagine a sparkling early morning in July, sitting on a harbour wall in the depths of Devon, waiting for your boatman and scanning the quiet water for signs of mackerel – a popular bait for larger fish. Or picture a lonely estuary on the south coast, in August, as the first of the ebb tide turns your boat slowly around on its anchor. You wait, excited yet contented, passing time in the peaceful solitude, until the bass leave their feeding grounds on the mud-flats, to swirl downtide, perhaps to take your waiting bait or lure and ripping line from your reel in a first mad dash for freedom.

Bass, those powerful hard-fighting torpedoes of the inshore waters, their strong flanks covered with hard silvery scales that glisten as the fish comes, at last, to the waiting landing net. Yes, many sea anglers are completely addicted to bass fishing, and the reasons, once you have caught one, will not be difficult to understand.

Later in the year, when the typical fish of summer have left the quiet, warmer waters, and sharp north-easterly winds blanket the shingle and breakwaters with white frost, you could find yourself standing on a cold winter 'storm' beach, dressed for the part in a thick sweater and fur-lined parka, anticipating the first thrilling jerk of the rod tip that will signal the bite of a good cod, far out under the iron-grey, foam-crested rollers.

All of these things and many more go to make up the rich pattern that is sea fishing; the constantly changing weather, the inevitability of the seasons; huge, wide-mouthed cod – or slim little whiting; a hooked bass streaking through the surf, or the incredibly powerful tugging of a great conger eel, a hundred feet down in the mysterious barnacled hulk of a forgotten wreck.

But, like other types of fishing, sea angling can be hard and unrewarding. Quite often, you'll spend eight hours in a biting wind, waiting patiently for a shoal of cod, and, with numbed face and fingers blue with cold, give up at last, swopping cold and discomfort for hot drinks beside a warm fire. Then, after several such unproductive trips, you'll begin to wonder if February cod fishing is really worthwhile – worth all that trouble and discomfort. But the call of the sea will be strong, next weekend will probably find you there again, determined to make this particular trip a real red-letter day. For fishing is like that, it's a constant challenge, a poignant uncertainty, a never-ending battle with the raw elements, and, above all, there is the 'end product', the pursuit of fish – even when you know the odds are in favour of the pursued!

Bank on it, though, your day will come – it will all happen. At the third, fourth or even fifth fishing trip, everything will suddenly be *right*. In the car on the way home, with your face stinging with robust health and satisfaction – and possibly with some good cod tucked away in a plastic bag in the boot, you will have found the ultimate answer; yes, it *is* worthwhile – every blessed minute of it.

The very fact that you are reading this book means just one

thing. Deep inside you there's a gentle, compulsive stirring towards becoming a sea fisherman; an almost irresistible urge for the lure of wild, unknown places and the plaintive, lonely call of seagulls.

Like most worthwhile things in life, the attractions of sea angling are numerous, yet, please be warned, so are the dangers. The sea is, at best, an uncertain friend and, at worst – a relentless and very dangerous foe.

So for all of you who are poised, anticipating the delights and attractions of angling in the sea, we feel obliged to stress – emphatically – that at all times, safety *must* be the keynote, particularly when fishing from an open boat in rough weather. Fortunately, many experienced boatmen are available to you, and in our experience, their word should always be law – they know when, or not, to take out a boat and their advice invariably stems from years of hard experience in their own areas. For your own sake, take their advice – every time.

To press this point even further, we can recall several occasions in the past when, after motoring many miles to a distant shore in the bleak early hours, we arrived, only to find that the offshore weather had deteriorated, and our kindly but prudent boatman's philosophy was 'Have a go from the pier, if you like – but I'm not taking you afloat in *that*!'

Hard as it might seem, after such an early start and so much tiring travel, his advice was always heeded – without question. Similarly, fishing from the beach or shore can have its hazards. A calm summer's evening, for example, can lull you into a false sense of security, particularly when visiting unknown coastlines in such apparently tranquil places as the West Country. The temptation to explore quiet coves and beaches is very strong, but, even in such idyllic places, the tides can be treacherous and you might find your only means of retreat cut off, without any obvious warning, by the unseen tide surging quietly across the sand or rocks behind you.

Clothing, too, is a very important item for the serious sea angler, as the balmy weather of a summer's day can so often change to penetrating cold, after dark. Later in this book, we give specific advice on the appropriate clothing for sea fishing, particularly when venturing out to sea in winter. So, always remember that the sea, sometimes calm, sometimes rough, is your adversary – and presents real dangers to the uninitiated.

Of course, no fishing can be learned entirely from books, but we hope that in the pages of this book, you will find the *basic* knowledge that will help you catch good fish from shore, boat or pier and, in addition, give you sound instruction in the right type of tackle and baits – and how to use them to good advantage. But, most importantly, we hope you will glean some useful information from the accumulated knowledge of experienced anglers, knowledge that will not only help you with your fishing, but will also help keep you safe, at all times, when you go fishing in the sea.

For, like most pursuits that are spiced with a hint of danger and excitement, sea angling is inordinately absorbing, adventurous and demanding. It's a man's sport in every way.

1 Tides and the shore

Many beginners to sea fishing, particularly those living well inland, tend to 'graduate' from lake and river fishing; consequently,
their first introduction to angling in salt water can be bewildering.
In comparison with a slow-moving river, or a placid pond, the
sea, from a fishing point of view, seems to be one vast expanse of
water, often completely featureless, stretching for mile after mile
to the distant horizon, with little or no immediate indication of
where the fish are to be found.

The second big difference between the sea and inland fresh
waters is the tides. We consider this second point so important to
the beginner that, we are going into it in detail in a moment. Whatever you do, don't skip this information, however technical it
might appear at first glance, for an understanding of tides and
how they work is the vital key to successful fishing around our
coasts.

Getting back to the vastness of the sea for a moment, the beginner might be tempted to 'chuck it and chance it' by convincing
himself that, with all that water, the fish must be somewhere – 'So
why not where I cast my bait?' What we hope to show you, in
this book, is how you can 'read' the physical characteristics of a
stretch of beach, or the sea bottom around a pier or breakwater,
or immediately under a boat, then to link this knowledge with an
understanding of the various fish that inhabit different types of
territory. This will be followed up with details of the baits, tackle
and fishing methods for catching most of the varieties of fish that
can be found around Britain's shores. But, bear with us for a moment, and let us get down to some really serious information
about tides.

Tides

From the sea angling point of view, the most important thing about tides is that they can, once you know how they work, actually predict the arrival, or departure, of feeding fish from a particular spot.

As we all know, tides are caused by the pull of the moon and sun on the seas around the earth. When the sun and moon happen to pull in line with each other, we get a condition known as 'Spring Tides', which is, in fact, a condition of the highest high water and the lowest low water. Don't be confused with the name 'Spring' tides, as these tides will occur, not only in spring, but approximately twice a month throughout the year. The high water at this time is known as High Water Spring (HWS), and as you would suspect, the low water is known as Low Water Spring (LWS).

So it follows that if, during a Spring Tide, the highest high water and the lowest low water occur then the greatest range between high and low water will be experienced. A vast volume of water will flow into a given area, and out again, over the period of that tide, causing strong tidal streams. The very highest tides will normally occur during what are known as the Vernal and Autumnal Equinoxes, around 21 March and 23 September, when the sun is directly over the equator, producing its most powerful influence on the tides.

When the sun and moon's gravitational pulls are opposing each other, they have an opposing influence on the tides, causing a condition known as the Neap Tide, when the lowest high water and the highest low water occurs. These tides are known as High Water Neap (HWN) and Low Water Neap (LWN), and as the range between the two is at its shortest, they give rise to slack tidal streams. In general, the amount of water flowing during a Neap Tide is about half that of a Spring Tide.

Spring and Neap Tides will occur approximately week and week about (to quote a good seafaring term), with a slight variation in tide condition each day, so that conditions will exist when tides will be falling to Neaps or rising to Springs.

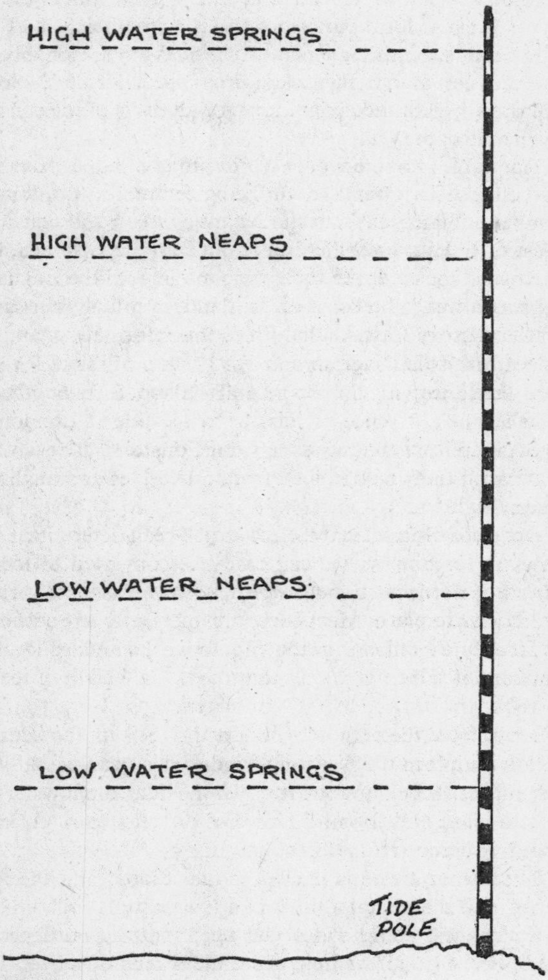

HIGH WATER SPRINGS _ _ _ _

HIGH WATER NEAPS _ _ _ _

LOW WATER NEAPS _ _ _ _

LOW WATER SPRINGS _ _ _ _

TIDE
POLE

figure 1 Tide heights

Another point to remember is that irregularities in the sea bottom can cause local variations, both in the height and rise and fall of a tide, but, as a general rule, tides are reasonably predictable and can always be looked up in special Tide Tables, which will show general tide conditions for all parts of the coast, at any given time of the year.

Tide tables for the whole world are computed from standard ports, those for Great Britain being centred on London Bridge. The tidal influences from the Atlantic Ocean will reach the west coast of Ireland first, then surge out into the Irish Sea, from the north and south, at the same time moving up the English Channel and around the coast of Scotland, eventually meeting again off the shore of East Anglia. From this information, and with the help of the Tide Diagram on page 17, you will find, for example, that Penzance, in Cornwall, and Ullapool, in Scotland, both have a time difference of tide, from the tide at London Bridge. This difference is known as a Tidal Constant, as it never varies, and can usually be obtained from tide tables and angling magazines.

Once your local Tidal Constant has been determined, the tidal times at London Bridge can easily be converted to local times. This does not apply to tide *heights*, however, as these vary, widely, from place to place. Most harbours, piers, etc., are equipped with a 'Tide Pole', which is graduated above a standard level or 'Datum' and it is from this pole that the actual height of the tide can be read.

Apart from the pull of the moon and the sun, the tides can also be affected, locally, by strong winds, which can actually 'hold' a tide on the shore, by slowing down the tidal ebbflow. In the same way, a wind blowing in the reverse direction can 'cut' a tide by speeding it away from the shore.

The rise of a tide is known as the 'Flood' and the fall is the 'Ebb', and the period at high and low water is called the 'Slack'. The strongest tidal flows occur where natural bottlenecks affect the water, a good example being the Straits of Dover, where all the tidal flow to and from the southern part of the North Sea is constricted into a relatively narrow channel. In the same way,

figure 2 Flood tidal streams

wherever the flowing tide is pushed through a narrow entrance, such as a river estuary or harbour entrance, the tidal flow will be affected accordingly.

Although the 'mechanics' of tides is technical to almost being dreary, we're glad you have followed us this far, because once we know the characteristics and causes of tides and tidal patterns, we can reap the benefits as anglers, for, make no mistake, tidal knowledge is the means by which the feeding patterns of sea fish can be predicted.

Take beach fishing, for example. As a general rule, when the tide rises *up* the shoreline, the fish follow it up, to feed upon the newly flooded sand, and shingle. And here's a good tip. Very often, the best beach fishing is to be had when the rising tide coincides with dusk, giving the fish the added security of approaching darkness. There are exceptions, however, as you might find that your favourite beach fishes best at *low* water, as the lowest edge of the tide makes accessible, for fishing, some vital fish food source such as a mussel bed, or a warm patch, that can't be successfully reached during a higher tide.

Just to illustrate how widely tide conditions can vary around different parts of the coast, you might leave your 'low water' beach fishing and travel a few miles to an area where the tidal flow is such that, while at one phase of the tide the fish are kept feeding well offshore, at another they are feeding close inshore. Therefore, never take any stretch of shore for granted, but always seek the golden key to successful fishing – local knowledge, usually to be readily obtained from men who have spent a lifetime studying and adapting to their own local conditions. Local angling clubs, books and individual local fishermen should all prove to be excellent sources of information, but without doubt, the finest way to gain real knowledge of your own is to concentrate on one spot, for as much time as you can spare, and glean its secrets and (with luck) its delights, at first hand.

Tides can also be extremely useful to the angler, giving access, at low tide, to parts of the sea-bed that he will actually be fishing over; allowing a fine opportunity not only to collect bait (worms, crabs, etc.) but also to conduct an intricate study of the nature of the bottom, helping him to decide what type of tackle and methods to use when the rising tide brings the fish to his waiting bait. Very often, a stretch of apparently featureless sandy beach will reveal, at low tide, several slight depressions, vital 'nooks and crannies' that will furnish feeding fish with an attractive few more inches of water in which to browse and feed. Shingle beaches, too, can often reveal projecting points, around which the swirling tide might collect concentrates of food to interest the foraging fish. Later in this book, we shall be discussing how to obtain bait from beaches at low tide; how to look for the concentrations of lugworm, ragworm, mussel and razor fish that make one particular stretch of shore that much more attractive to feeding fish.

So, whenever you can – on a week's holiday to the coast, for example – always search for the tell-tale signs that separate the good fishing spots from the bad or indifferent. Get out at low tide and study the bottom, carefully, as every minute spent in this way could reap great dividends. But again, be warned – the sea has a nasty habit of creeping up behind you, so watch the effect of the tide at your rear, and don't ever make the mistake of getting cut-off, with the awful possibility of an uncomfortable (fully clothed!) wade or swim to dry land.

The shores around the British Isles vary, in their physical nature, and for fishing purposes we have simplified them into five basic types. This is only intended as a rough guide, however, and please remember that all five variations could occur within a mere few hundred yards of any one coastline. We will break these variations down into the following:

1 Hard rock
Look for cliffs with fragmented rock below them; also heavy growths of weeds below the tide level. Another usual feature of this type of shore will be the typical 'rock pools' we all explored, at some time, when we were children at the seaside. In many hard rock areas, very deep water can often be found close in-shore. Typical hard rock areas around our coasts include parts of Devon, Pembrokeshire, Yorkshire and Scotland.

2 Soft rock (chalk and sandstone)
These rocks also give rise to cliff formations, but with the difference that the shoreline below will be smoother, often with patches of sand or shingle and occasional ridges of soft rock. The chalk

shores of Kent and the sandstone coastlines of Dorset are good examples.

3 Shingle banks

Shingle, which is merely rock formed into various sized 'pebbles' by the continual ebb and flow action of the tides, will usually be found where tidal flows are strong, or where long, narrow areas of rock project out to sea, coming into contact with the action of the tide. Classic examples include Chesil Beach in Dorset, Orford Ness on the Suffolk coast and Dungeness in Kent. Here, great ridges of shingle are formed by storms and tides and they are usually favourite haunts of beach-casting anglers, who hunt the fish that love the rich feeding to be found on the bottom of the submerged shingle.

4 Sand

Generally, these areas present large, flat expanses of sand, unbroken by rock or shingle, where the tide often retreats a long way from the shore. Because of their featureless nature, they are probably the most difficult areas for producing angling, but, as already mentioned, it is sometimes possible, at low tide, to discover some irregularity in the pattern of flat sand that could indicate a good fishing 'mark'. Flat sandy beaches are numerous around the coasts, and a list of the more obvious ones would be too long to describe here. A good ordnance survey map should tell you all you want to know.

5 Mud

Mud can be found in most river estuaries, at the bottom of harbours and in dock entrances. It will usually provide good feeding ground for most sea fish, and will attract numerous small crabs, other crustaceans, various varieties of worms and other food attractive to fish. But, here's yet another warning. Please be *very* careful when exploring areas of muddy shore – and take special care when wandering over mud flats at low water; this substance is usually very soft, and the unwary bait collector or explorer might find himself, suddenly, right up to his hips in smelly black ooze – with little or no help at hand!

Now, having discussed the mysteries of shores and tides, our next task is to become familiar with the real object of the exercise – the fish that are to be found around our shores, in summer and winter.

2 The angler's sea fishes – their haunts, food, season and weights

Not the least of the attractions of sea fishing is the wide variety of fish to be found around our coasts, each species offering its own particular attractions – and challenges – to the angler.

For the fisherman dedicated to the use of light tackle, there is the hard-fighting bass; while, at the other end of the scale, huge conger eels are to be discovered lurking in deep, forgotten wrecks and sea-bed crevices, only to be captured with the help of really heavy, strong tackle – which, on occasions, will be tested to the limit. Then there is the shark hunter, drifting along the calm sum-

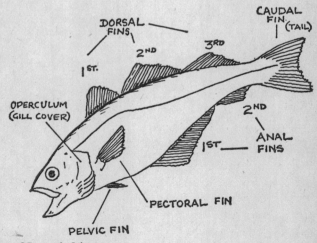

figure 3 Parts of a fish

mer surface in his shark boat, scanning the water for signs of his quarry, the blue shark, porbeagle shark or the 'big one' – the ferocious mako.

It's all a question of scale, and whilst the thrills and adventure of really big fish hunting must be attractive to the beginner, we would offer a word of sound advice. Don't be tempted to try your hand with the 'big stuff', right away. Start nearer the bottom of the scale and cut your teeth on the smaller fish – then graduate to bigger things.

In this chapter, we are describing the more common fish that the beginner will be likely to encounter; it is by no means a complete inventory of all the British sea fishes, and is not intended as such, but, in the main, should be regarded as a 'starting' list for those who are new to the game and who wish to start their fishing by tackling the more obvious species.

Some of the terms we must use to describe the various fish might appear to be a little complex to the novice, and to assist you, please refer to the sketch on page 22 as a general key. Now to the fishing. Let's imagine that, because you are just starting, you will probably choose the summertime, for obvious reasons; so we will commence with the fish of summer, starting with one of the easiest summer fish to catch, the mackerel.

figure 4 Mackerel

Mackerel

Characteristics
A beautiful streamlined fish, marked with irregular vertical dark blue bars along its handsome green back.

Haunts

Will more commonly be found, in shoals, in the surface layers of the open sea, but in summer will often shoal, in large quantities, closer to the shore, even around piers, etc. The mackerel, which is extremely nutritious – and good to eat – will give an unforgettable account of himself if caught on fairly light tackle.

Food

The mackerel's food consists mainly of minute sea creatures, sand eels, and the eggs and small fry of other fish such as herrings and sprats.

Season

Mainly found inshore, during the months of summer, and will normally depart for deeper offshore water in the winter.

Weight

Usually in the region of $\frac{3}{4}$ lb to 1 lb (340 to 450 g), a 2 lb (900 g) fish being a reasonably unusual specimen.

figure 5 Cod

Cod and codling

Characteristics

The cod has three dorsal fins and two anal fins, all with distinctly rounded edges; the head and mouth are large, in proportion to the whole fish, but the eyes are small. The cod's lower jaw is shorter than the upper, and sports a single 'barbule' or feeler, which is a characteristic of many bottom-feeding fish. The general colouring of the fish varies, but is generally sandy brown on the back, with mottled brownish marks to the sides. Look also for the typical white belly. Codling are simply smaller cod, under 5 lb (2.25 kg) or so.

Haunts
Cod can be found all around the coasts of Britain, from the shoreline to deep offshore marks, and once found, will usually be in good-sized shoals, except for the larger specimens which tend to hunt in small groups of two to five in number. Some of the really heavy 'rod-benders' will frequent the areas around deep-water wrecks offshore, sometimes taking a bait meant for other fish.

Food
Cod have been described, on one occasion, as the 'dustbin' of the sea-bed; they will, in fact, eat practically anything! To illustrate this point even further, we know of cod that were caught, complete with several white plastic cups in their gullets! In the main, they will tend to feed off the bottom, when close inshore during the tidal flow, but will normally inhabit the upper water layers during slack water.

Season
In Britain, the cod is mainly a winter species, although the odd fish can be encountered when fishing wrecks or rocky marks during the summer. In recent years, large catches have been made, on rod and line, from the English Channel banks, the Varne being a particular favourite.

Weight
It is a known fact that cod over 150 lb (68 kg) in weight exist – they have been netted, on occasions, by professional fishermen.

But before you get too excited at the prospect, remember that the average rod angler can be justly proud of a 20 lb (9 kg) fish and extremely pleased about a ten-pounder.

figure 6 Pouting

Pouting

The pouting, a member of the cod family, is known, in different parts of the country, by various names – 'bib' and 'whiting pout', for example. Pouting are smaller than cod, but have similar fins. To spot a pouting, look for a black spot between the gill-covers and the pectoral fin; also its coppery-coloured back with four or five darker vertical bands, and the large eyes. Found all around our shores, mainly on sandy bottoms, the larger pouting will also inhabit solitary rocks or wrecks. They will feed on shrimps, small crabs and other small sea creatures, sometimes proving to be a nuisance when devouring, with great relish, larger baits intended for more worthy fish. They seldom reach more than 3 lb (1.4 kg) in weight, an average fish being more likely to weigh ¾ lb (340 g) to 1½ lb (680 g). *Note*: once killed, pouting will deteriorate very quickly; consequently, they're not regarded as a good fish for the table, but are used mainly for processing into fishmeal.

Whiting

Another member of the cod family, the whiting is a predatory fish – hence its small needle-sharp teeth. It can be identified by its streamlined shape, sandy-green back and silvery white sides; also, the upper jaw is longer than the lower one, and the chin has no barbules – unlike the other members of the cod family. The whiting is quite a good sporting fish, particularly when caught on light tackle, but in most cases will usually be taken on heavy cod-fishing gear, when it will obviously give a poor fight. Whiting are very common all around the coasts of Britain, the shoals usually coming inshore in early autumn, and for anglers, herald the arrival of the cod. Whiting feed mainly on small fish, shrimps, prawns and hermit crabs – almost anything, in fact, that is small enough to devour. *Note*: when unhooking a whiting, have respect for its teeth; you might not sustain any serious injury, but after a successful day's whiting fishing, you could suffer from 'whiting finger', a series of small, painful scratches around the upper joints of the index finger and thumb. A 4 lb (1.8 kg) whiting would be exceptional, the average weight being around 1 lb to 1½ lb (450 to 680 g).

figure 7 Whiting

figure 8 Pollack

Pollack

Characteristics
Although, strictly speaking, the pollack is yet another member of
the cod family, it is regarded, by anglers, as a fine sporting fish, reaching much larger weights and putting up a more
spectacular fight than both pouting or whiting. Look for the dark
brown back, shading sharply to golden yellow flanks and a lightish
yellow belly. The pollack's lower jaw protrudes beyond the upper,
and the chin has no barbules.

Haunts
Pollack are mainly fish of rocky coastlines, particularly in the
south and west of the country. Smaller pollack can be found close
inshore, whilst the larger fish prefer rocky reefs and wrecks.

Food
The main food of adult pollack consists of sand eels, rock-
dwelling fishes, blennies, wrasse, rockling, prawns, shrimps and
crabs.

Weight
Pollack caught from sunken wrecks often exceed 20 lb (9 kg) in
weight, while those from rocky shorelines usually weigh up to
about 5 lb (2.25 kg).

Season
Throughout the year.

Coalfish

Characteristics
One of the larger members of the cod family, it is also known as
Coley or Saithe, its back and upper flanks being of a browny-
green colouring, with silver-grey lower parts. The lower jaw protrudes, slightly, beyond the upper, and there is a small barbule on
the tip of the chin.

Haunts
All around our rocky shores, but particularly in northern waters.
Smaller coalfish are shoal fish, the larger specimens tending to be
solitary or in small groups.

Food
For the smaller coalfish, food consists mainly of tiny marine
creatures and the small fry of other fish. Larger specimens feed
almost exclusively on other fish such as herring, whiting and small
cod.

Weight
Fish over 20 lb (9 kg) are exceptional and are usually taken from
deep water. The smaller shoal fish usually range from $\frac{3}{4}$ lb to 2 lb
(340 to 900 g).

Season
Throughout the year.

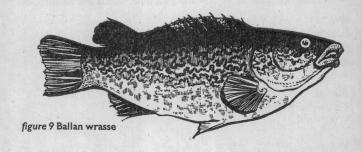

figure 9 Ballan wrasse

Wrasse

The various members of the wrasse family are described below, and for the sea-fishing beginner, will be easily identified, owing to their highly coloured markings, thick lips and small, heavy teeth – designed for tearing shellfish from the rocks and crushing small crabs. All the wrasse have sharply-spined dorsal and anal fins, and a thick, heavy 'wrist' to the tail.

Ballan wrasse: the most common of the British wrasse family, green or greeny-brown in colouring, with reddish back and white markings on the lower fins and belly.

Cuckoo wrasse: male: bright blue head and back, with yellowy-orange flanks; female: pinkish-red, with three darker spots to the back, behind the long dorsal fin.

Corkwing wrasse: a mottled greeny-brown, with blue and orange marking to the belly and under the head. Many corkwings have a dark spot at the root of the tail.

   Whilst this list does not represent all the wrasses to be found around our shores, the three described will be the most commonly caught.

Haunts
Wrasse enjoy the rocky, weed-strewn waters, often very close to the shore. The smaller fish will usually be caught very close in-

shore, in rocky gullies and at the sides of stone jetties and harbours. The larger wrasse can be found close to the shore, but prefer the deeper gullies slightly offshore.

Food
This consists mainly of small shellfish, barnacles, limpets, mussels, crabs and tube worms. Wrasse will also act as scavengers, even raiding crab and lobster pots for the bait they contain.

Weight
Ballan and corkwing wrasse can, on occasions, be over 5 lb (2 kg) in weight, but the cuckoo wrasse, a much smaller fish, seldom reaches much more than 1 lb (450 g).

Season
Found inshore at all seasons, although wrasse will be more active feeders in the summertime, retiring to deeper water as the weather ecomes colder.

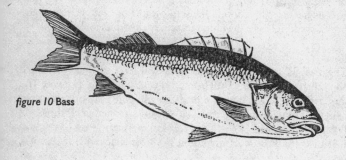

figure 10 Bass

Bass (*Salmon bass*)

Characteristics
We do not hesitate to suggest that the bass is one of the finest sporting fish in British waters – salt or fresh. This long, streamlined and heavily scaled fish, with its sharp, spiny dorsal fin and

spiny gill-covers, has a grey-blue back with handsome silvery sides and a creamy-white belly. Catch your first bass, and you'll be most impressed with how firm and muscular it is to the touch; it is truly a beautiful and hard-fighting fish, by any standards, and because of its popularity with anglers, its numbers are, or soon will be, under 'pressure', since it is a very slow-growing species, taking, generally, some twenty years to reach a weight of 9–10 lb (4–4.5 kg). If you get 'hooked' on bass fishing – as we are sure you will – please do everything possible to preserve the species; whenever possible, always return your bass to the water and take a tip from the really dedicated bass anglers, who only take the occasional bass 'for the pot'.

Haunts
Mainly inshore and lovers of the river estuary, harbour entrance, tide rips around banks or rocks offshore – anywhere, in fact, that supports a fast tidal current. Fresh water too, will attract the bass, and they are frequently known to travel well up the lower reaches of rivers, even to almost completely salt-free water. Try for your bass as he hunts his food in the shallow inshore waters, just as the tide is 'making' over the mudflats and rocky foreshores.

Food
The bass is strictly a predator and will feed savagely on most small fish, also squid, cuttlefish, sand eels, crabs and prawns. The larger the bass, the bigger morsel he will enjoy; one bass, when caught, contained two cuttlefish weighing together 1 lb 12 oz (795 g), and he was 10 lb 14 oz (4.94 kg) in weight. Fish of this size will also think little of engulfing a whole mackerel of about a pound.

Weight
By all means set your sights on a 10 lb (4.5 kg) bass, but he will be an exceptional specimen; catch a six-pounder and you'll have the envy of the locals. When immature, the bass will shoal in large numbers, usually consisting of fish between ½ lb and 1 lb (225 and 450 g), sometimes known as 'checkers'. Unfortunately, these little

checkers are wantonly abused by so-called 'anglers' who kill large numbers just for the hell of it.

Season

Mainly summer, but occasional individual fish are caught in the winter, particularly from warm water outlets of cooling plants and power stations.

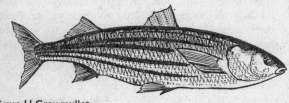

figure II Grey mullet

Grey mullet

Characteristics

There are several species of grey mullet, the most common being the thick-lipped type, and the one most unlikely to be encountered around the shores of Britain is the golden mullet. All species have very similar shapes; a four-spined dorsal fin and a secondary dorsal fin with soft 'rays'. The grey mullet can be easily identified by the long greyish bands running from head to tail along the back and sides, with a blue-grey back and silvery-coloured flanks. The thick-lipped mullet has a wide upper lip, whilst the thin-lipped mullet (another sub-species), has a much more narrow upper lip. The golden mullet, which also has a narrow upper lip, has distinctive golden marks to the head and gill-covers, but this fish will rarely be encountered in British waters.

Haunts

The grey mullet loves the brackish (salty-fresh) waters, and on occasions will even be found in purely fresh water, swimming alongside chub, roach and dace in rivers such as the lower Hampshire Avon. Look for them in harbours and places where the tide is not too strong – and you'll discover these handsome, hardfighting fish foraging for food around the weed hanging from moored boats, pontoons or bridge piles.

Food

Mullet feed mainly upon plant life and small shellfish such as seed mussels, small slipper limpets and similar marine creatures; they will also eat the young of crabs, shrimps and prawns, etc. Occasionally, the mullet will be tempted to take small worms, and maggots that inhabit rotting seaweed lifted by a particularly high tide.

Season

Mullet are essentially a summer species, feeding freely almost exclusively in the summer months, though a particularly warm autumn might tempt them to feed.

Weight

Thin-lipped and thick-lipped mullet have been caught by commercial fishermen up to almost 17 lb (7.5 kg) in weight; but, generally speaking and as far as the average sea angler is concerned, a fish of 4 lb (1.8 kg) or over is a very worthwhile specimen. As mentioned previously, the golden mullet is a smaller, much more rare fish, and a 1 lb (450 g) fish would be a specimen.

Black bream ('Old Wife')

Characteristics

This popular sea fish is, in appearance, deep-bodied, with a fairly small head and small, sharp teeth. The body colouring is silvery, with attractive dark blue vertical bars along the back and sides. The fish is quite heavily scaled, and has a solid, chunky look about it; it is also quite powerful for its size and will prove himself a sporting opponent on suitably light tackle.

Haunts

Black bream only come to British waters to spawn, and this they will do mainly around the rocky ridges off our southern coasts. When visiting our shores, this bream is fairly widespread, and an odd small black bream can be caught almost anywhere, in the season, from Land's End to John o'Groats. In the main, however, the largest concentrations will usually be found off the south coast of England – principally in the months of May and June.

Food

Although little is known about the actual feeding habits of this fish, its mouth and teeth strongly suggest that its principal food consists of small crustaceans and small fish.

Season

Essentially a summer visitor to British shores, although it is not unknown for a small black bream to be taken in winter.

Weight

A black bream over 3 lb (1.4 kg) in weight can be considered a good fish, whilst one of 4 lb (1.8 kg) or more is a specimen.

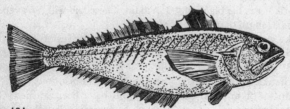

figure 12 Lesser weaver

Weever (*Greater and Lesser*)

Although the marine waters of most tropical countries contain many fish and plants that are dangerous to human life, the temperate seas around the coast of Britain are more benign, and there are very few dangers to be encountered by the casual swimmer, angler or paddler – apart from the odd stinging jellyfish that swims off the south coast in hot weather. There is an important exception, however – the weevers. These fish are armed with venomous glands at the base of the spiny dorsal fin, and on the spines of the gill-covers. Please take great care when unhooking one of these fish, as a wound from these spines can produce extremely painful symptoms that could persist for up to twenty-four hours. In extreme cases, a weever sting can be even more dangerous, so, if you should be unfortunate enough to get stung, always seek medical help as soon as possible.

Characteristics
The body shape of the lesser weever is short and tapered, with distinctive eyes positioned at the top of the head. The mouth is large in proportion to the body, and slants sharply upwards. The dorsal fin is small, with four spines (these are the ones to watch!) and there is a secondary dorsal fin which, like the anal fin, is long and almost reaches to the tail. The gill-covers, too, have spines, and like the ones on the dorsal fin, must be avoided when unhooking the fish. In general colouring this fish is yellowy-brown on the back, shading to a lighter buff colour at the sides. Another point to look for is the black first dorsal fin. These fish will, on average, attain a length of up to 7 in (18 cm).

The greater weever, while it is similar to the lesser, has a proportionally longer body and the eyes positioned at the sides of the head; also, the back is of a greyish colour, shading to yellowy-buff flanks. Like its cousin, this fish also has poisonous spines on the dorsal fin and gill-covers, so – you have been warned! The greater weever will normally reach a maximum length of up to 15 in (38 cm).

Haunts
In normal conditions, the weevers will lie on a sandy sea-bottom with only their eyes and dorsal fins visible, and, in view of their poisonous nature, it is fortunate that only one variety, the lesser

weever, is to be found close inshore; the greater weever being generally a creature of the deeper water.

Food
The weevers feed mainly upon the small marine creatures that inhabit the sandy sea-bed; small fish, worms, etc. *Note:* the weever will quite often be caught when fishing for flatfish like the plaice and sole, and if one is captured, hold it underfoot (not bare feet, please!) and either quickly rip out the hook or remove it with pliers or forceps. Even when dead, the weever can still inflict a painful sting, so be extra careful at all times.

Weight
The average maximum weight for the greater weever is about 2 lb (900 g).

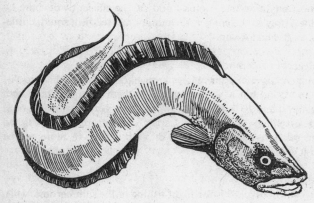

figure 13 Conger eel

Conger eel

Characteristics
There is something of the legendary 'sea serpent' about this long, powerful eel, and once you have tussled with a good one, even on

robust tackle, you'll be blessed with an enduring respect for its brute strength and dogged tenacity. It has no tail fin, as such, but sports a long dorsal and anal fin which runs along the whole body, coming to a point at the tail. The pectoral fins (just behind the gills) are pointed. The conger's head is equipped with large, powerful jaws, and the eyes – which usually peer balefully from some subterranean crevice or pipe, are large and oval. In colouring, the conger is browny-black, with greyish sides and a white belly.

Haunts
Smaller conger eels prefer the rocky ledges and gullies close to the shore, while the larger specimens can best be hunted in deeper offshore water – sunken wrecks being a favourite haunt.

Food
Almost anything that swims – and can be efficiently devoured – will fall prey to the conger, including most sea fish, squid, cuttle-fish, crabs and lobsters.

Weight
Commercial trawlers have been known to net congers in excess of 100 lb (45 kg) but if you're fishing for them from the shore with rod and line a 20 lb (9 kg) fish would be a very worthwhile (and muscle-aching) proposition. Larger conger are usually fished from offshore boats and an eel of 50 lb (23 kg) or more can be considered a specimen.

Season
Our own preference is for night fishing in the summertime, when the better eels seem to feed. These fish dislike severely cold wea-ther, and will retire to deeper water as the winter approaches.

Silver eel

This is the well-known smaller 'freshwater' eel that migrates, in summer, to the Southern Atlantic, and will often be caught by sea anglers in river estuaries and very close inshore. It can be distinguished from the younger conger eel by the rounded pectoral fin and small round eyes. Will sometimes reach a weight of around 3–4 lb (1.4–1.8 kg).

Garfish

Characteristics
Easily identified by the long, beak-like jaws and slim, elongated body. In colouring, it has a brilliant green-blue back, with silvery sides.

Haunts
More commonly found in the surface layers of our inshore waters in summertime.

Food
Generally, the garfish lives on the smaller plankton and the small fry of sprats, mackerel and herring.

Season
A common summer visitor, the garfish will usually depart as autumn arrives – destination unknown! Since there is little commercial value to this fish from the food point of view, very little is known about its winter migratory habits.

Weight
Will usually reach about 1 lb (450 g) in weight, a fish of 2 lb (900 g) or more being exceptional.

figure 14 Garfish

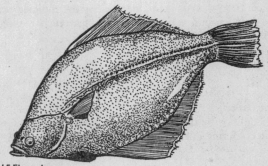

figure 15 Flounder

Flounder (*or Fluke*)

Characteristics
One of the smallest members of the flatfish family, the flounder's eyes are positioned to the right-hand side of the body. Follow the lateral line along the body, and where this meets the gill-cover, small knobs or tubercules can be found. Similar tubercules can be seen at the base of the dorsal and anal fins. Flounders vary in colouring, according to habitat, but generally, the upper side will range from a greeny-brown to a dark olive, with a white underside. Both upper and under sides may be marked with a series of dark blotches.

Haunts
The flounder favours muddy or sandy bottoms around river estuaries, moving, quite often, right up into fresh water.

Food
The principal food of the flounder consists mainly of small immature shellfish, crabs, shrimps and various marine worms.

Season
Although flounders are present around our shores during the

months of winter – and can be caught during that time, their main
feeding period is during the warmer months of spring and summer.

Weight
Usually, rod-caught flounders will weigh around 1 lb to 1½ lb
(450 to 680 g), a fish of 3 lb (1.4 kg) or more being a real feather
in your cap!

Sole

Characteristics
Several types of sole are present around British waters, the common or Dover sole, Sand sole, Variegated sole and the Solenette.
In all these species, the anal fin runs from the tip of the jaw almost to the tail; the dorsal fin too almost reaches to the tail. The
eyes are on the right-hand side of the head, and the mouth is
small, curved and extremely strong. The scales of the soles have
a rough 'sandpaper' feel to them, and in general body colouring
these fish have brownish-grey upper sides and off-white under-
sides.

Haunts
Found close inshore during the summer months, the sole is mainly
a nocturnal feeder, usually lying semi-buried in sand or mud
during the daytime. In winter, it will normally retire to deeper
water.

Food
Like most flatfish, the sole feeds principally upon small shellfish,
small crabs and worms, etc.

Weight
An average weight for this fish is around 1 lb–1½ lb (450–680 g), a
sole of 3 lb (1.4 kg) being an exceptional specimen.

Plaice

Characteristics
The dorsal and anal fins of the plaice reach almost to its tail, and
the eyes are on the right-hand side of the head. In colouring, it is a
rich brown, with distinctive large orange-red spots, the underside
being of an almost white hue.

Haunts
The plaice loves sandy bottoms, also mud and occasionally shingle
or shell territory. The smaller plaice are caught mainly inshore,
during summer, while the larger fish are to be found offshore,
sometimes near to mussel beds.

Food
High on the plaice's menu are the small shellfish, mussels, whelks,
cockles, etc., but they will also feed upon marine worms, sea
mice, starfish and very small fish of different species.

Weight
Expect your plaice to be between 1 and $1\frac{1}{2}$ lb (450 to 680 g), as
a general rule. Land one of 4 lb (1.8 kg) or more and you have
a specimen.

Dab

Characteristics
Brush a dab from front to back – and you'll immediately discover
how rough it is to the touch. Other recognition points include the
dorsal and anal fins, running almost to the tail, while the eyes are,
like other species of flatfish, on the right-hand side of the head.
The general colouring is brown, with mottled markings, and,
occasionally, white spots on the upper side. The underside of the
dab is white.

Haunts
Shallow, inshore waters, the general preference being for sandy bottoms, where it lies or forages for food. The dab will move into deeper offshore waters during severe winter weather.

Food
A greedy feeder, this dab: in fact, he'll devour almost any small living marine creature that reaches his field of vision.

Weight
The dab, being the 'baby' of the flatfish family, rarely reaches a weight exceeding 2 lb (900 g). Even a fish of 1 lb (450 g) is a good one!

figure 16 Grey gurnard

Gurnard

Characteristics
There are several types of gurnard in British waters, the three most common being the Yellow (or Tub) gurnard; the Red gurnard and the Grey gurnard.

In all three, a good recognition feature is the 'separated' front three rays of the pectoral fins, which are free of any membranes. With these 'feeler' fins, the gurnard searches out and sifts his food on the sea bottom. All the gurnards have heavily 'plated' heads and rows of spiky spines over body and head. In general colouring, these fish can be identified as follows:

Yellow (or Tub) gurnard: pinky-brown back and sides with creamy-white belly. The pectoral fins are red, with distinctive blue spots.

Red gurnard: red all over, with pale, rose-coloured underside.

Grey gurnard: blue-grey body, occasionally with a pinkish tinge to the sides. The underside is off-white.

Haunts
The Yellow gurnard is normally found throughout the southern coastal waters of the British Isles, preferring the open sandy or gravel bottoms in deep water. The Red gurnard is mainly a fairly deep water fish and is not too fussy about the type of sea-bottom he inhabits. This fish can be caught around most British coastlines. The Grey gurnard has no preference for depth, and can be found equally widespread throughout inshore and deeper off-shore water. Whilst it will normally prefer sandy or muddy bottoms, it can sometimes be located quite near to the surface, according to climatic conditions.

Food
As we have already mentioned, the gurnards forage for food with their specialized 'feeler' fins, and will unearth a wide variety of creatures concealed in the sea-bed; crabs, shrimps, small fish, cockles, mussels, sand eels – almost anything, in fact, they might find.

Weights
Yellow gurnard, anything over 8 lb (3.5 kg) is an extremely good fish. Red gurnard: a two-pounder is a specimen. Grey gurnard: try to break the current record – which stands at 1 lb 1 oz (482 g).

Season

Mainly a fish of the summertime, often hooked while fishing for other species, although the occasional gurnard will be taken during mild winter weather.

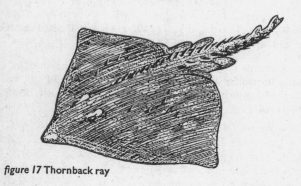

figure 17 Thornback ray

Thornback ray (Roker)

Characteristics

Known to anglers as 'skate', the thornback ray lives up to its name, having a row of 'thorns' right down the centre of its upper side, and along the tail. Small clusters of these distinctive thorns can also be found on the 'wings'. In general colouring, this ray has a grey-brown speckled upper side, with the underside white.

Haunts

Found around most parts of the British coasts, moving on to sandy or muddy bottoms, in shallow water, when coming inshore to spawn. Sometimes, in winter, good thornbacks can be taken from the deeper offshore marks. In summer, the distinctive 'sachet'-shaped egg cases of the thornback can be seen scattered along the shoreline.

Food
Mainly large shellfish, crabs and a variety of fish – all of which will be tackled with the powerful, crushing jaws of the thornback.

Season
Thornback rays love shallow water, preferably with a muddy or sandy bottom, and, in the spring, will move inshore to breed. As they usually come in pairs, if you catch one you will often catch its mate soon afterwards.

Weight
Although thornbacks are caught to weights of 30 lb (14 kg), an 18–20 lb (8–9 kg) fish is a good one, the average fish being around 10 lb (4.5 kg).

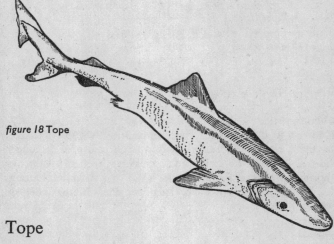

figure 18 Tope

Tope

Characteristics
The tope is one of our smaller native (British) sharks, and, like the sharks, is a truly sporting fish at the end of a line. Beautifully streamlined in shape, with a grey back, shading down to a grey-white belly. This fish, like its near cousins, has extremely sharp and dangerous teeth – so please, handle him with care at all times.

Haunts

Wide open, larger areas of shallow water (like the Wash, for example), usually with a sandy or muddy bottom, where the tope can chase and 'run down' its food.

Food

True predators, tope will chase and devour many different varieties of other fish, principally whiting, codling, pouting and flatfish. In summer, they will also attack and decimate the shoals of mackerel that come to the shallow inshore feeding grounds.

Season

Spring usually heralds the arrival of tope in the type of waters described above and once they arrive, they will normally stay for the spring and summer months, depending on the weather. Tope activity will also increase with the coming of the mackerel shoals in summer, but, as the weather turns colder, the tope will move offshore, becoming increasingly more difficult to catch.

Weight

A good, average tope weight will be roughly between 17 lb and 23 lb (7.5 and 10.5 kg). You will do extremely well to catch a forty-pounder, but, just to whet your appetite, they can actually weigh over 70 lb (32 kg).

Dogfish

The four types of dogfish listed below are the ones the British sea angler will be most likely to catch. In shape and general characteristics, they all resemble the sharks and have the unmistakable shark-like 'undershot' jaws.

Spurdog: in colour, this one is dark grey, with pale coloured spots on the back and sides, and is easily identified by the sharp spines on the two dorsal fins – which also make him a dangerously difficult fish to handle. Please be careful!

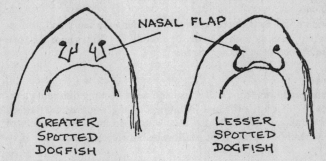

figure 19 Dogfish identification

Greater-spotted dogfish (*Nurse Hound or Bull Huss*): this 'dog' has a sandy-brown back with white spots, and a white belly.

Lesser-spotted dogfish (*Sandy Dog or Rough Dog*): similar, in colouring. but can best be distinguished by studying the nostrils and nostril-flaps (see fig. 19).

Smooth Hound: a dull greyish-coloured back, with a creamy coloured belly. Although there are two definite species of smooth hound, they are so similar that an expert would be needed to make an authentic identification.

Haunts
All the dogfish described can be found around the coasts of Britain, and, in the main, prefer to do their serious feeding on, or near, the bottom.

Food
You name it – the 'dogs' will eat it, from fish, crabs and lobsters to prawns, squid, etc., dead or alive!

Season
Generally, summertime is the time for 'dogs', as, during this warmer period, they will move inshore to feed in earnest. Don't be

surprised, though, if you connect with one in deeper offshore waters during other parts of the year.

Miscellaneous species

The list of angler's sea fishes we have described in this chapter are the principal ones that you, as a beginner, will be more likely to encounter. Of course, there are many more, mostly smaller, rather insignificant fish – from the angler's point of view. These species include the Blennies, Rocklings, etc., which we shall be covering in the next chapter, and describing the various baits. In addition, we have, for obvious reasons, omitted several fish like the larger flatfish, the Turbot and Brill, which are somewhat 'specialized', from the beginner's point of view. These two fish are caught mainly from shingle banks, offshore, and are mainly fish eaters. Other fish include the Horse mackerel, or 'Scad', a bony fish, with little sporting – or eating – value, which is usually found, and caught, where mackerel are present.

Then there is the Angler fish, a hideous, flat, ugly, multi-toothed monster that preys upon other fish, and can hardly be considered as an angler's delight! Other fish that can, on occasions, be caught around British shores, are the Monkfish, various Rays, including the Cuckoo, Blonde, Spotted and Sting rays; the Shads, Lumpsucker, Sunfish, Catfish, Dragonet – and many more, all of which can best be described as the 'odd men out'. Don't bother with them, but concentrate on the more obvious, catchable fish instead. On the other hand, if you should catch one of these 'less likely' fish, study them and admire the wide diversity of nature's spectrum, and, apart from the big flatfish we have mentioned, which are very good to eat, please, return them, unharmed, to the water – they are of little use for the table, but, in their natural habitat, have a job to do. So, get into the habit, from an early stage, of returning unwanted fish to the water. To kill natural and living things, just for the sake of it, is barbaric – and far too much of it is going on today, as man depletes the wondrous harvest of land, sea and air – without regard for the eventual consequences.

Finally, we have purposely left out the obvious 'big game' fish, like the Blue, Porbeagle, Thresher and Mako sharks; also the large Common skate and the lordly Tunny fish – the largest fish to be caught in British waters. We sincerely hope that, in time, you will 'graduate' to the catching of these large and immensely powerful fish, all of which will require a distinctly different approach, in terms of tackle and angling methods, to those already described. Please, get to know the sea – and its more common fishes – more intimately, first, 'cutting your teeth' on them, improving, all the time, your skill and knowledge, until, eventually, you feel both confident and competent enough to tackle 'bigger game'.

Now that we know, in some detail, what we are after, let's take a closer look at the baits on which these fish are to be caught.

3 Sea angling baits – where to find them and how to keep them

Baits always present a real and lasting problem to the average sea angler, particularly if he lives some distance from the sea. Strangely enough, bait appears to be in plentiful supply when few fish are about, but a sudden – and frustrating – shortage can occur when the fish start feeding in earnest.

The coastal angling shop with a significant crowd of anglers around the door is usually a good sign that the fish are 'in', and the demand for bait is great.

By far the most popular sea fishing bait is the marine worm, in one form or another, principally the ragworm and lugworm. In the main, these worms are dug by professional bait-diggers, who collect the worms to order and despatch them to the bait shops as soon as possible. At some time during his angling career, the average sea fisherman will try digging his own bait – and it is only then that he will come to realize that the professional digger earns his money the hard way!

Since bait is such a problem, let us take a closer look at these much prized marine worms, and, for the angler who wishes to be 'independent' where bait is concerned, suggest how to dig for them with some reasonable measure of success.

Lugworms usually live in sand – or a mud/sand mixture – on clear, open beaches, and if you walk across the sand at low water, you're bound to observe small heaps of sand looking, for all the world, like small piles of sandy spaghetti. These heaps are the 'casts', the sand that the lugworm has passed through its body and pushed out on to the surface of the sand. Nearby you'll see a small conical depression at the bottom of which will be a small hole. This hole marks the 'head end' of the worm, giving the bait digger a good indication of the direction in which the worm is lying. To capture your worm, take an ordinary garden fork and place the prongs parallel to the line between the hole and the cast, and about 9 in (23 cm) away from them. Then push the prongs firmly, to their full depth, levering the sand upwards out of the hole, then turn it over.

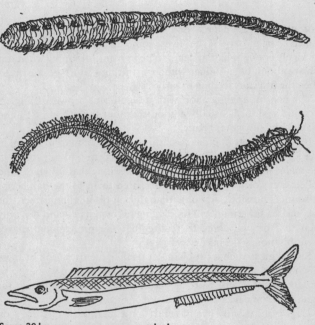

figure 20 Lugworm; ragworm; sandeel

The lugworm should then be visible and can be gently removed from the sand. If, however, you don't spot him right away, then you should carefully examine the sand you removed from the hole, and if you see part of him, break open the sand to expose him. If this process fails to produce your lug, take another forkful from the same hole and repeat the process from the beginning.

Lugworms collected this way can be stored by spreading them out on clean dry newspaper, in a cool (but not cold) place, such as a concrete garage floor, making sure you don't pile the worms one on top of the other. These worms tend to exude a quantity of natural liquid, so use several layers of newspaper to absorb this moisture. Next, cover the worms with another sheet of newspaper, and – this is most important – change the paper at least twice every day, morning and evening, for example, as the fastest way to lose your worms is to leave them in sodden paper.

Ragworm can be dug in a similar way to lugworm, from muddy beaches at low water mark, the big difference being that, unlike the obliging lugworm, your ragworm will not leave any surface indication of his presence. In the main, the ragworm loves to work under mussel beds, or in areas where the sand is mixed with shell or shell shingle, and this is where the professional ragworm digger will look, digging in the likely spots until one or two worms come to light, then digging, methodically, in an outward spiral, throwing the dug-out sand into the centre of the hole. In this way, they can cover an obviously productive area, moving systematically through the 'good patches'.

To store ragworms (once you have caught them), wash out the sand or mud in sea water and pack them in a wooden box, preferably on a layer of fine washed gravel taken from the beach. Finally, cover them with a further layer of gravel. As an alternative, they can be wrapped, individually, in newspaper – and here's the best way to do it. Lay the first worm on the lower edge of the sheet of newspaper and roll it up until it is completely wrapped. Do the same with the second worm – and so on – until about two-thirds of the sheet of newspaper has been used, which, by this time, should contain roughly five worms. Then fold the edges of the roll of newspaper inwards, at the same time rolling up the complete 'pack'. In this way, each worm will be firmly encased in newspaper, separated from its fellows, and packed in a good 'escape-proof' container.

The ragworm comes in a variety of sizes, the smaller ones being known as 'harbour' rag, each worm being about 3 to 5 in (8 to 13 cm) long. The larger ones are known as 'king' rag and will often be found to a length of 12 in (30 cm) or more. This size ratio can be a good guide to the type of worm you are buying at your bait shop, the size acting as a good indication of whether you are getting value for money or not.

Unfortunately, due to the tremendous upsurge in the popularity of sea angling in recent years, bait is becoming scarce, and the professional worm digger is continually searching for new bait grounds – as his livelihood depends upon it. So, if you should discover a particularly good and productive source of lugworm and ragworm, keep it to yourself – or, the next time you fancy some bait for your own fishing trip, you might find the supplies exhausted.

Before we pass on to other types of sea fishing baits, some reference should be made to the 'white' ragworm. This is a smaller variety of ragworm, creamy white in colour, and generally found when digging for larger lugworm. Although it is somewhat small and 'delicate', this white ragworm is an extremely good bait, so much so that its use is forbidden in many sea angling competitions. So, if you should come across this white rag, when digging for other bait, don't throw it away – it could make the difference between a fishless day and a full fish-box.

Quite often, when you're out digging for marine worms along the mudflats and beaches, you will discover other types of natural baits along the seashore. Many different creatures will be found, sheltering under rocks, lurking in rock pools, or washed up along the tide-line, and these 'bonus' baits will very often prove extremely useful when you're out fishing and the fish are difficult to tempt. The principal baits to be found in this manner are:

Slipper limpets

These shellfish are often washed ashore by rough seas; they are true shellfish, each shell being formed like a 'slipper', the fish itself acting as the 'foot' inside. Usually, these shellfish will stack themselves one on top of the other, like cricket caps on an umpire's head, until there are six or eight together, each one stuck firmly to the shell of the other. Because of this, they have been jokingly referred to as the 'flat dwellers' of the sea.

To obtain an excellent bait, for several types of sea fish, simply prise the two shells apart and use the slipper limpet's body on your hook. These 'stacks' of limpets can also be kept, for quite long periods, in dampened seaweed, each bait taken for the hook, as required.

Razor fish

These shellfish live mostly in sand, and are to be found at the lowest spring low tide and beyond. In shape, the shell is like an old-fashioned 'cut-throat' razor, hence the name, and they live in a vertical tunnel formed in the sand, which is shaped like a keyhole. When searching the sandy beaches for bait, look for the 'keyhole' and you should find your razor fish. These holes are not easy to locate, but once you have done so, take the customary razor fish digging tool – which is a long, barbed spear of thin steel, and push it down the 'keyhole', hopefully penetrating the razor fish, then turning the spear through a quarter-turn to engage the bottom edge of the shells, after which the fish is gently pulled out of the hole.

Razor fish caught in this way should be used for bait very quickly, as they soon deteriorate once out of their natural habitat. Another way of catching razor fish is to go around putting salt on their tails! Unbelievable, yes, but quite true. You simply arm yourself with a typical drum of table salt – and pour a little down each razor fish hole. In theory, the whole process is quite plausible, as the huge increase in salinity proves extremely uncomfortable to the razor fish, and it will 'pop up' to escape the extra saltiness.

If you catch your razor fish this way, always wash them, right away, in sea water, to rid them of the high salt solution. To keep them in good condition for fishing, put them in a box, covered with seaweed, and they will remain fresh for several days. To prepare the bait for fishing, remove the long, slender shell from the fish, leaving the tough white body, which is an excellent bait.

Mussels

These can be found on rocks, harbour walls, pier piles and similar places; and we feel sure you have seen many of these creatures when exploring under piers at the seaside. The larger mussels make a good sea fishing bait, but great care must be taken when opening them. Usually, a short-bladed knife is the best tool for the job, and this is used to sever the leathery 'hinge' and cut the meat from the shells. This meat consists of a yellowy-orange piece, with a black 'tongue' at the end, and since the body of the bait is soft, the hook should always be inserted in the tongue, otherwise the bait is inclined to fly off when casting. Some anglers even tie the bait on the hook with elasticated cotton thread, particularly if casting long distances.

Cockles

These bivalves are to be found in sand, but normally would only be used for bait when other baits are difficult to find. To gather cockles, rake them from the upper level of the sand and place them in a bucket, then pour boiling water over them, after which the shells may be opened and the small pieces of flesh removed for bait. Cockles will often make a good bait for flatfish like plaice and dabs, but are not to be recommended as the ideal bait.

Limpets

These, again can be regarded only as a 'desperation' bait, and can be found quite easily, adhering securely to rocks. They can be collected by giving the shell a sharp sideways tap with a hammer or rock, or prising the suckerpad away from the 'home' rock with the point of a knife.

Clams

Several types of clam can be found, usually when digging for marine worms. The shellfish vary in size quite dramatically, the larger ones being an excellent bait for cod in wintertime and thornback rays and flatfish in summer. Open your clam with a knife, using the tough white body inside as the bait.

Crabs

Other typical baits found along the seashore include crabs, the most common one being the shore crab, which is green in colour, with a pale underside. This crab has two different guises, the soft-shelled type, or the 'peeler' type, which has shed its shell. The angler will get to know, love *and* hate this creature, for he is, all rolled up into one, a truly great sea fishing bait, and also a greedy voracious scavenger who will, without compunction, nibble and eat almost any bait that the angler puts on his hook.

With all due respect to this animal, which, after all, is only a link in the complex chain of nature, we must explain that, for some eleven months of the year, the shore crab is a crawling 'dustbin', eating anything and everything in sight – including the angler's baits, acting as an uninhibited nuisance to anyone who plies rod and line in the sea. But about twice a year, the crab out-grows its shell, and goes through a process of casting off the old shell, gradually growing a new one to replace it. At this stage, he tends to desist from his bait-scoffing exploits and becomes, in-stead, a bait supreme!

For, underneath the outgrown, soon-to-be-discarded shell there is, being formed, a velvety-soft, new shell waiting to take its place, just a size larger than the old one. Eventually, the old shell will be cast off, leaving behind a perfect replica of the old shell, but considerably more soft in texture, as hard, in fact, as an over-ripe tomato! Since, at this stage, the crab is extremely vulnerable to predatory fish, he will hide away until his new shell hardens sufficiently to give adequate protection. Quite often, he can be found secreted away underneath a 'hard' crab – so bear this in mind when looking for him.

This peeler crab, because of his softness for hooking – and his attractiveness to fish, makes a really good bait for many different types of sea fish.

When looking for crabs among the rocks, under seaweed, or in the low-water-exposed debris of the harbour bottom, you will find other types of crab, mostly shore crabs, but sometimes the edible or swimming varieties. The soft crabs, however, can be easily recognized, as once the shell has been shed, they will lie still and make no 'threatening' motions with their claws – as normal hardback crabs will do.

He's quite easy to collect, at this stage; simply pick him up gently and pop him into a cloth bag or plastic bucket. At the pre-shedding shell stage, the peeler crab is quite difficult to spot, but the experienced bait collector will immediately notice the 'old' look to the shell, perhaps even with a barnacle or two attached to it. However, for the beginner, here is an easier method of identification. Hold the crab in the right hand, with the index finger and thumb spanning the shell – to prevent the beast from clamping its claws into your lily-white skin! Then, take the lowest joint of one of the walking legs between the finger and thumb of your other hand – and break it off (the leg, not your finger!). It should come off quite readily, so, now for the moment of truth. If, as the leg is broken off, meat is revealed underneath, then you should apologize profusely to your crab and return him to his lair, but, and keep your fingers crossed, if the brown, velvety-smooth imitation of a lower joint comes to light, keep him – he's a peeler!

And here's another tip; don't ever keep peelers and softies together in the same bait container, as the peelers will quickly proceed to damage, kill and eat the unfortunate soft ones. To prepare your peeler crab for the hook, kill him by exposing the vent (under the body flap) and pierce, with a sharp point, through the vent, into the body. Once he is dead, lift the main shell from the back edge, gently, until the complete shell is off, exposing the soft velvety skin below. The bait can now be hooked and bound, just like the 'softy'.

Crabs can be kept, as bait, for short periods, but the natural process will continue; the softies will get harder and the peelers peel and become softies. In the main, a good wooden box fitted with an efficient lid and filled with damp seaweed is all that will be needed to keep crabs.

You've probably already heard of the 'hermit' crab; this is a variety that 'camps out' or 'squats' in the disused shells of whelks and other shellfish. These crabs have a soft tail that requires constant protection, as the creature moves house, from shell to shell, as the living accommodation becomes too cramped. Hermit crabs are usually to be found in rock pools, and can often be caught with the aid of a 'drop net'. This is quite a simple type of net, fixed to a length of cord, baited with bits of fish and lowered to the sea-bed from a pier, harbour wall or a boat. Once you have removed the hermit from his protective shell, he is fairly soft and will make an excellent bait.

Prawns and shrimps

Can be caught in the same way, and are also very good baits, particularly if fished on float tackle for bass, pollack, etc. If you have any left over, at the end of the day's fishing, and providing they are still fresh, they make a good 'man' bait, too!

Small fish

At low-water mark on a typical rocky shore, a wide variety of small fish can be collected for bait; hence the old expression 'a sprat to catch a mackerel'. Among these are blennies; a small fish usually found in shallow water. They have blunt heads, and, for their size, quite large teeth. The general body shape is tapered sharply to the tail, which is small and stubby. They have a long dorsal fin, reaching almost to the tail, with an anal fin to match, and they move in distinctive quick darting bursts over the sea bottom, feeding upon tiny shrimps and crabs.

There are several varieties, the best known being the butterfish or gunnel, which has a long, slender brown body, speckled with regular black spots along the back, at the base of the dorsal fin. Another shallow-water fish is the goby, which is similar, in habits and location, to the blennies. Again, there are several varieties, all with two dorsal fins, the first one having six 'rays' – and very sharp they are too! Small eels, another good bait, at times, can usually be taken (with some difficulty!) in rock pools and similar places – if the eyes and fingers are nimble enough for the task.

Other small bait fish that can be caught by the sea angler are smelts; a beautiful silvery, green-backed fish that, surprisingly, exudes a distinctive odour of cucumber when handled. These small fish can even be caught on rod and line, using very small pieces of fish or shrimp as bait. Used whole, they will make an extremely good bait for bass and pollack.

The young of most fish – such as pouting, pollack, sprats,

whitebait and bass, etc. – can sometimes be found among the rock pools and mudflats, and can always be used as bait for larger, predatory fish of the same, or different, species. They can be used, live, or kept in the deep-freeze to be utilized later when bait might be scarce, mounted on suitable dead-bait tackle.

Sandeels

The sandeel is widely known as a really prime bait for several different types of fish but, unfortunately, is difficult for the beginner to obtain. The professional bait collector usually gets his sandeels either by using a special fine-meshed net, or by 'raking' for them in the sand at low-water mark. The most efficient way to keep sandeels, alive, is to put them in a floating, perforated wooden box, usually called a 'courge'. Most sea anglers purchase their sandeels, in frozen form, from their bait shop, but, if at all possible, we recommend that you use them live, and, failing this, very fresh. There are two distinct species, the lesser sandeel and the greater sandeel, or 'launce'. The launce can occasionally be caught with a set of small feathered hooks, jerked up and down in front of the sandeel shoal.

Mackerel can be caught in a similar way; not a particularly sporting method of fishing, but nevertheless, a good way of filling the bait box, at times. The mackerel, one of the most free-biting and obliging of all the sea fish, makes an excellent bait, either fished whole, for the 'big game' fish, or filleted and sliced for more general-purpose angling. Because of its free-biting and shoaling tendencies, this fish is much abused by some 'anglers', who, upon finding a shoal of these quite pretty, blue-striped silvery fish, proceed to massacre them in countless numbers, and far in excess of their culinary requirements. After the slaughter, when the shoal has departed, some thirty or forty beautiful mature mackerel are piled in the boat to be dumped back into the sea, unwanted and useless.

So please, if you're lucky enough to catch up with a good shoal of mackerel, only kill or take away those fish that are genuinely needed for the family table. If every angler did this, the diminishing harvest of the sea could be conserved, for a little extra time, at least. The 'lecture' now being over, there are still a couple of good fish baits about which you should know.

Garfish

These fish can often be found close to the mackerel shoals, and can prove to be a very good bait. Being slender in shape, and silvery in colour, the garfish can be chopped into long lengths to make a big bait, providing a good area of attractive, silvery surface to marauding fish of the larger species.

Herring and pilchards

These soft-fleshed fish are not the ideal hook-bait, but have great attraction to predatory fish (and crabs!) owing to the rich, oily juice they release.

Squid and cuttlefish

Here's a case of 'last, but not least', as both these fish provide an excellent general-purpose bait. They can be fished whole (according to their size), or cut into strips. These interesting fish, which, incidentally, are close relatives of the octopus, can now be purchased from the fishmonger or bait shop, in frozen form, as certain elements of our immigrant population consume them with great relish. The small Chinese or Californian squid make excellent large baits for cod, bass or conger eels, usually fished whole.

The large squid or cuttlefish, caught by our own trawlermen, are only used cut into strips, or the head and tentacles are used as a large bait.

As a general rule, most baits should be clean and fresh-smelling, to be successful, but, on occasions, a really 'high' bait, that needs to be put on the hook at 'arm's length', will lure a specimen for you.

Once you have gleaned considerably more experience as a sea angler, many more different types of bait will be revealed to you, but, as a beginner, the aforementioned list should suffice. Now, having covered the question of bait, we will concern ourselves with the next very important facet of sea angling – tackle.

4 The sea angler's tackle

For the raw beginner to sea angling, one of the most bewildering places in the world will be the tackle shop. These shops vary in size and contents but, if he happens to pay a visit to one of the larger, more comprehensive shops in a typical city, the very complexity and volume of the different items of tackle displayed, all having their specific purpose, will seem like a 'nightmare'.

So, let's immediately try to simplify matters, to give you a good, preconceived idea of what to look for and how to purchase wisely; for, like any other kind of shopping today, the accent must be on value for money, which we can assure you will vary widely.

As a basic principle, always go to a good, specialized fishing tackle dealer: the man behind the counter is almost certain to be an angler himself – and, in consequence, in a first-class position to give you sound, unbiased advice. Try it. Approach one of these good tackle dealers with an open mind. Tell him, right away, that you know nothing – you're in his hands. What would *he* advise in terms of tackle and methods for your first fishing holiday on, say, the Dorset coast. Don't pretend to know *a little* about it, but come clean. You're just starting – don't know a lugworm from a rubby-dubby bag; could he help equip you, at minimum cost, for two weeks' fishing from beach and boat, with particular emphasis on the fish that (he will know) are most common in that part of the world.

He'll love you! Here's a man, he'll say to himself, who doesn't pretend to be an expert, but *genuinely* wants advice and help. So, put yourself in his hands. A word of warning. Don't go, for your advice and tackle, to one of the big 'chain stores', which usually have a small department dealing with fishing tackle. You're very likely to encounter some smart 'dolly bird' whose main interests are pop-stars and boy-friends, and whose basic knowledge of fishing leaves something to be desired. Unfortunately, she is more likely to sell you anything that comes to hand.

Another good, basic principle, when purchasing fishing tackle, is only to buy the best that you can afford. Don't, under any circumstances, buy 'flash' gear, or 'gimmicky looking' tackle. They are usually cheaper, but, in the long run, will not last; so, avoid them.

Always pay particular attention to the metal fittings on rods and reels, and always go for stainless steel or chrome-plated. Remember, it is the performance and durability of fishing tackle that counts, not its appearance. Cheap dural fittings, for example, might look good and shiny in the tackle shop but, after a few weeks' exposure to salt water, will tarnish and corrode appallingly.

Now, to start at the very beginning, let's take a look at what will probably be your first fishing 'outfit', a rod and matching reel for beach fishing.

Rods

Most modern fishing rods are now made from glass-fibre, or, to quote its proper technical title, glass reinforced plastic (GRP). These rods are available in two basic forms, solid glass and hollow glass, the solid glass producing strong, inexpensive rods, which usually have the disadvantage of being heavy. Although these rods might feel quite reasonable to hold, in the tackle shop, their extra weight will impress itself upon you, in no mean fashion, after a good, average day's fishing. Nevertheless, in spite of weight, many anglers still use solid glass rods – and swear by them. For our part, however, the extra money spent on a hollow glass rod (for they do cost quite a bit more than solid glass) is well worthwhile.

For beach fishing – that is, casting a baited hook, line and weight from the beach or shore – the fishing tackle maker classifies his rods into 'casting weight' classes, usually 2–4 oz (57–113 g), 4–6 oz (113–170 g), and 6–8 oz (170–227 g), the weight quoted being the most appropriate casting weight range for the particular rod. When you go to choose your own beach-fishing rod, bear in mind the nature of the shore you will be fishing, particularly the strength of the tide, for this will usually determine the 'class' of rod you require. In the main, however, and because of lightness and ease of handling, the novice will usually be better off with the 4–6 oz (113–170 g) rod, to start with.

Another type of beach-casting rod on the market is the 'fast taper' rod, made to cast weights of 3–9 oz (85–255 g), and in which the glass 'blank' is designed to produce the casting 'action' in the higher part of the rod, to give great power and speed for longer distance casting. At this stage, we would advise you to avoid these long-distance rods, attractive as they might seem, for they are not really beginner's rods and will almost certainly require a great deal of practice and acquired technique before a long, smooth cast is achieved.

So, having decided what type of rod you require, turn your attention, now, to the rod fittings. The rod rings (for passing the line through) should be of a good quality, for maximum wear and value. The best ones, in our view, are the hand-chromed metal rings or, alternatively, those with pink ceramic material linings. Rod rings really do take a lot of hammering over an average year's fishing, particularly beach rod rings, which have to contend with continual heavy-duty casting, where the line carries a 'film' of very fine shingle matter, picked up from the beach and sea bottom. This matter is extremely abrasive and will produce damaging 'grooves', especially in the top ring. So, buy the very best you can afford.

In the same way, the other metal rod fittings are prone to corrosion by the steady action of salt water – unless, of course, they are well protected. The best ones are either made from stainless steel, or chromed brass. Some of the cheaper rods will have anodized aluminium fittings; avoid them, if you can, for eventually they will corrode badly. The other rod fitting material used today is plastic, but again, this varies in quality, according to the price of the rod.

Another point to watch, when buying a rod, is the 'whippings', the bindings that hold the rings to the rod. These should always be well varnished to keep out rust and weather, and, if you should get a rod that in all other respects is a good one, it is a fairly easy job to add a few extra coats of varnish to the whippings.

The most important factor in the choice of rod has been left, deliberately, to the end. This is the length of rod. Many beginners to fishing – and even some more experienced anglers – believe that the length of the rod is the golden key to successful distance casting; and off they go to buy rods of 13 ft (3.2 m) or 14 ft (4.3 m), hoping for instant success. Let us impress this point upon you; the best length of rod is the one that suits your *physical build*. If you're a five-feet-tall (150 cm) seven-stoner (50 kg), the most likely thing you will achieve with a 14 ft (4.3 m), 4–6 oz (113–170 g) rod is a double hernia! However, if you are 6 ft 4 in (194 cm) and weighing a (healthy) 16 stones (116 kg), then you're in with a much better chance of using these larger rods with some effect.

Most average-size adults can handle a 12 ft (3.7 m), 4–6 oz (113–170 g) rod fairly comfortably, but younger people are well advised to commence with a 10 ft (3 m), 4–6 oz (113–170 g) rod. Remember also, when looking for a rod, that it must be suitable for the task you will be asking it to do. Fishing for summer bass, for example, will need a good, lightweight rod, capable of casting some 2–4 oz (57–113 g), whereas, in comparison, fishing a winter 'storm' beach will need a much more robust tool, particularly as in this type of fishing weights of up to 8 oz (227 g) must be cast at long distance.

Another point to consider when buying a rod is the distance from the 'butt' (thickest) end to the point where the reel fittings are fitted. This distance, ideally, should be just over your shoulder-width apart, to allow a good natural stance when holding the rod in a horizontal position across the chest. Watch for this, as some rods are produced with an extra-long butt-to-reel distance, making them very difficult to use for the beginner.

Materials used for the handles of rods are cork, rubber, plastic and cord. All these materials produce quite a good grip, particularly plastic, and most sea rods are made today with plastic hand-grips. Cork is the warmest material to hold – a point to remember when you must hold a rod, for hours on end, on a cold February cod beach.

Generally, sea rods require little maintenance, apart from an occasional lubrication of the ferrule or spigot (the joint of the two rod lengths). Also, keep a careful watch on the rod rings, and check every so often for signs of wear. Like most other items of sea fishing tackle, your rod will benefit greatly from a regular wash down after use, and will last you longer. Simply take some warm fresh water on a soft sponge, and work well into the threads of the reel fittings, to remove the salt crystals that have collected there. Then wash the rest of the rod, paying particular attention to the handle where traces of bait and fish scales will be adhering. Finally, give a quick wash down of the whole rod and let it stand in a warm place to dry. If your rod-bag got wet on the beach, wash this, too, in fresh water, but *don't* put the rod back in it until it is perfectly dry. If you look after your rods in this way, they should last for many years, and only require a new set of rod-rings, as the old ones become grooved with continual wear.

This 'grooving' will be particularly evident in the top ring, for, when you are casting, the fine grit adhering to the line will act like a fine file on the metal! Make a point of thoroughly checking your top ring after every fishing trip, for, once it begins to groove, the line will take to that one convenient 'channel', and the ring will wear very quickly.

Most glass-fibre beach rods are extremely tough, and with a little basic care such as we have advocated, will prove to be almost unbreakable; even so, care must be taken in their method of storage. Always store your rod by hanging it up by the loop that is fitted to one end of the rod-bag, but take care *where* you store it. One angler we know leaned his prize rod up against the garage wall, and as he drove his car out one misty morning it fell down – under the car wheels. This incident did absolutely nothing for his rod, or his temper!

Reels

Reels for beach casting are many and varied, and most are made in the UK, USA, France and the Far East. They fall into two

main types, the 'multiplier' and the 'fixed spool' (see illustrations).
The fixed spool reel has a forward-facing fixed spool, housed in a
rotating 'head', to which is attached the 'bale arm' for controlling
the line. This bale arm can be opened manually and locks back,
allowing the line to flow freely from the spool when casting. The
first turn on the reel handle will close the bale arm as it sweeps
the line into the roller, which, as it rotates with the 'head', winds
the line back on to the reel. While all this is going on, the spool
also moves backwards and forwards, laying the line evenly over the
spool, to ensure that the next cast will not be spoiled by a tangled
line.

Most fixed spool reels also have a 'slipping clutch' mechanism
that will allow a heavy fish to actually take line from the reel.
This clutch can be adjusted to the angler's individual requirements, but we will be describing this process in more detail when
we come to the part of the book dealing with 'tackling up'. One
other gadget on a typical fixed spool is the 'non-reverse' lever; a
mechanism that prevents the reel from letting out line when the
rod is put into its 'rest' on the beach.

Unlike the fixed spool, the multiplier reel has a horizontal,
very free-running spool and, consequently, requires an almost
completely different casting technique. The spool is so free-running, in fact, that *if it is not controlled* the line will over-run when
casting, causing an unenviable situation known as a 'bird's nest'.
Get one, and you'll immediately understand how it got its name!

Let's take a look at the 'controls' of the multiplier reel, beginning with the spool. This should be made from plastic, for lightness, and is positioned between the two end-plates of the reel.
When in position correctly on the rod, the multiplier will be *on
top* of the rod, with the end-plate containing the handle on the
right-hand side. This handle plate contains two controls; the
'free spool' lever and the 'star drag'. The free-spool lever is used
for connecting (or disconnecting) the spool from the handle drive.
When this is in the 'free-spool' position, the spool will run quite
freely on its own, and, at this stage, will require careful control,
to prevent 'bird's-nesting'. When the lever is changed over to connect with the drive, the problem of over-run is eliminated. You

will notice, also, that the handle will only wind in one direction, as the reel is fitted with an internal 'anti-reverse' device which allows the line to be *reeled in only*, and any line going out will only do so against the drag, which is controlled by the star-drag under the handle.

This drag can be set, by the angler, to prevent line from coming off the spool, under normal fishing conditions, but allowing a big fish to pull out line, thus preventing a break. The 'heavier' this drag is set, the greater will be the tension required to take line from the spool. Conversely, a 'light' drag can be set for lighter types of fishing. Now let's have a look at the other end-plate of the reel, the one opposite the handle plate. The only control, on this side, is a ratchet, to give some nominal tension to the line when putting the reel into free-spool, threading the line through the rod-rings – or untangling a bird's nest!

In our view, multipliers are by far the best reels for beach-casting. When you go to buy one, pick one with a wide, shallow plastic spool that is capable of holding at least 200 yds (185 m) of 20 lb (9 kg) line. Both fixed spool and multiplier reels will require washing, and occasional lubrication, after use. Usually you will get a maker's leaflet with your reel that will tell you how to lubricate, and how frequently. Always follow these instructions to the letter, and your reel should last, giving good loyal service for years. We know of one multiplier that is still running well, on a second set of bearings, after fourteen years of hard use, and is 'beside the seaside' at least three times a week, every week.

Lines

There are three basic types of line used for sea angling; the first – and most widely used – is nylon monofilament (monofilament simply means 'single strand'). This line is mostly used for all types of general fishing, from beach, pier or boat, but for the 'heavier' methods of boat fishing where one expects to 'pull' up heavy fish from deep, offshore waters, another different type of line comes into its own. This is the 'braided terylene' line, which is manufactured from terylene threads braided into a round, smooth line with minimum 'stretch'.

But be warned this line is inclined to be expensive and, as we have already advised you, please leave the 'big stuff' until later, when you have more experience. In a similar bracket is the 'wire' line, which is usually made from very fine diameter stainless steel strands, and is somewhat heavy in weight – so that, not only does it stand up to the stringent conditions of deep-water fishing but is also aided, by its extra weight, to get to the bottom quickly, particularly when a heavy tide is running and you want your bait fishing on the bottom as soon as possible.

These wirelines, for the beginner, are often difficult to handle because the wire tends to be very 'springy'; also, these lines usually need the employment of especially heavy-duty rods equipped with 'roller' rod-rings, to prevent excessive wear. Another important 'don't' regarding these wirelines – *never* use them for long-distance casting; this stuff is a bit like cheese wire, and, if you should, as a beginner, start casting with it – you could wind up minus a finger – it's that dangerous! So, please take note of what we advise – and avoid these lines until you feel qualified to use them.

So, let's get back to the most commonly used sea fishing line, the nylon 'monofils', and study them more closely. Monofil lines are available in many different 'branded' makes in a large variety of breaking strains and lengths. In our view, the most useful is the 2 oz (57 g) spool containing some 300 yds (275 m) of 18 lb (8 kg) breaking strain line. This is just about right to 'fill up' an average reel spool – and will avoid the muddle of, say, three separate spools of 100 yds (90 m) each, or, worse still, six spools of 50 yds (45 m).

A good principle when purchasing line is to avoid the very cheap stuff. Remember, you gets what you pays for! You're much better advised to go for a well-known, middle-priced line, and, once you find a brand you can trust, stick to it, loyally. If you feel inclined continually to 'chop and change' your line-brand loyalty, sooner or later you'll get a really bad line – which will probably lose you the fish of a lifetime.

When you do buy a line, whatever it is, always run the first few yards of the new spool through your fingertips – in the shop. If it feels rough to the touch, reject it, as this means it is either a bad make or has passed over a worn guide during its processing. So, be very choosy, remember that nylon line should be soft and smooth to the touch – and not too shiny. Also, choose natural shades of monofil; the dull greys, blues or browny-greys are best. In general, nylon is a strong, durable material impervious to water (in the short term) and cheaper to produce than many other materials; consequently, the beginner can try out his casting, with nylon monofil, knowing that a bad 'bird's nest' or two will not cut too far into his pocket-money.

But, again, a word of advice. While nylon lines need little or no attention, for general purposes, there is a basic rule that will prolong the life of lines – and keep them in good condition for fishing; sunlight is the enemy, and will deteriorate it very quickly, particularly if the line is left on a window sill, for example, exposed to bright sunlight for long periods. So, if you must keep your lines on the reel, or on their spools, be sure they are kept in a dark place.

Braided lines, as already described, are more expensive to buy because of the heavy cost of braiding the thread into efficient fishing line. These lines are used mostly in the higher breaking strains for heavier fishing; it is also used for spinning, on light 'multiplier' reels, a job for which it is well suited, owing to its softness of action on the spools of the lighter types of multipliers.

Lines, of every type, should be checked often for signs of excessive wear. Nylon, for example, tends to lose its surface, becoming paler in colour with use and exposure to the elements. Braided line, under the same conditions, can develop a 'hairy' surface, when the tiny ends of the worn fibres and wires start to 'strand'. This will show itself as odd needle-sharp ends of broken strands sticking out from the line. If you spot this type of wear in your line, remove the forward end, until you come to unworn line. After several such renewals, you will reach a point where not enough line is left for a safe reserve when fishing – and then is the time to invest in a new line.

Finally, it is essential that you 'load' your line on the reel in the correct way, to avoid undue 'twists and kinks'. Never load your line by letting it fly off the *edge* of the stationary spool; this will almost surely give you a twist in the line (on the reel) for every turn removed from the spool, causing endless trouble later, when fishing. The best method is to pass a pencil, or similar object, through the hole in the line-spool, connect the end to the reel backing line, then wind it on the reel, slowly, under a little tension if possible, so that the spool revolves as the line comes off.

Hooks

The next – and probably most important – item of tackle to be discussed is the hook, for of all the various items in an average angler's tackle box, the hook is the most neglected.

The novice angler's trouble usually starts at the tackle shop, and could go something like this:

Angler: I want some hooks.
Tackle Dealer: Certainly sir, what size?
Angler: Oh, I'm not sure, for cod and whiting, I think.
TD: Ah, you want 1/0s sir (produces a sample).
Angler: Oh no, bigger than that – and silver.
TD: What about these, sir, they're a 4/0 long-shanked fine wire, nickelled.
Angler: Umm, yes, I suppose they'll do.

Well, he's got his hooks, but let's have a good close look at what he's *really* got. Firstly, he wanted hooks for cod and whiting – which, early in the season, will usually 'run' together, so a specific size of hook wouldn't have been a bad idea, providing it was a *strong, forged* hook. Forging, in the trade, means that the hook has been strengthened, around the bend, by a process of flattening.

The fine wire hook the dealer gave him, eventually, size 4/0 would be much too large for whiting fishing, and may even be too weak for the larger cod, particularly in heavy tide conditions. Armed with hooks like these, the angler will soon learn the errors of his (and the tackle dealer's) ways, probably by losing some good fish. Also, when he gets back from the tackle shop, our angler will probably chuck his new hooks into a rusty tin box, no doubt in the company of some rusty old ones he has been 'bequeathed'. Very soon, under such primitive conditions, the new hooks will become as rusty as the old ones and just as unreliable.

So, please, if you buy new hooks, get a nice clean tin, or preferably, a plastic box, and line it with foam plastic material, 'Ethafoam' is ideal for the purpose. Then pull the point of each hook into the foam, setting the hooks out in groups according to type and size. Another good tip – don't put *all* your new hooks into the tin, simply take enough for a good day's fishing, plus a few spares; then, if a sudden wave, or shower, dowses your hook box, only a few will get wet, not your whole supply.

Another thing. Don't ever put oil or rust-preventive solutions on your hooks. Fish have an extremely keen sense of smell, and will fight very shy indeed of hooks tainted in this way. If you want to test the theory, put a few drops of petrol on a packet of bait, then go out for a day's fishing – and see what you *don't* catch! For the same reason, if you fish from a powered boat, be sure to remove all traces of oil or petrol from your hands, before handling tackle and baits.

Now, let's have a little 'anatomy' lesson on a typical hook.

The loop at the top of a hook is known as the 'eye', and the straight part down to the beginning of the curve is termed the 'shank'. The actual curved part is the 'bend', which will finally come down to the 'point'. The small tag of metal inside the point is called the 'barb'. A hook that has the point bent out of line with the shank is known as an 'offset', to give the hook a better chance of quick penetration. 'Forging' is a flattening of the bend, a process which thickens the steel in the direction of most strain; thus, a forged hook is stronger, generally, than an unforged one.

Hooks come in a wide variety of finishes; bronzed, nickelled and chromed being the most popular for sea angling. There are many other variations to the basic hook design, and two more common ones are the 'long shank' and 'barbed shank'. In the long-shanked

Night tide

A feather-caught mackerel is unhooked
Codling, whiting and pouting

John Metcalf's 136 lb (62 kg) halibut

Shore-caught pollack
A sinewy conger eel

Launching a small boat from the shingle
It's a beauty! A lesser spotted dogfish

Mackerel for bait

Big bass!

A really good bass surf is running

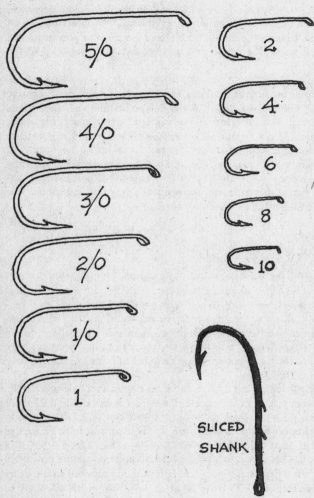

figure 21 Hooks

hook, the stem, or shank, is longer than usual, for better leverage, and with the barbed-shank variety, the small barbs are continued up the back of the shank, which have the effect of preventing the bait from sliding down, and bunching around, the bend of the hook.

To hook and hold fish efficiently, your hooks must be kept as sharp as possible at all times, as the continual action of abrasive rocks, shingle, etc., will dull the fine points in a very short time. The best tool for hook sharpening is a small sharpening stone, obtainable from your tackle or tool shop, and this is usually triangular in shape. Always sharpen the *inside* of the hook first, by gently 'stroking' the stone on each side of the bend, finishing with a fine upward stroke on the outside of the point. When fishing, repeat this process throughout the day and you should lose few fish through bad hooking.

Tackle

Now for the 'end' gear – all those various bits of tackle that can be so bewildering to the beginner, including the 'ironmongery' like swivels and wire. When starting, make simplicity your keynote – don't be tempted to construct weird and wonderful festoons of end tackles, but be basic; we're sure that, when you are more experienced, and know what you're doing, you will have endless fun – and possibly larger catches of fish – by evolving your own pet tackles.

For fishing from a boat, the most common tackle used is the 'flowing trace'. In this tackle, the weight is carried by a Clement boom, with two loops of wire, or a Kilmore link, with one loop of wire, both tackles sliding on to the main reel line. To fix this tackle, knot the end of the reel line (by a 'half blood' knot) to a swivel. This swivel will prevent the boom from sliding down any further. Then tie a separate length of nylon monofil to the other end of the swivel. This line is called the 'trace' which will have the hook, or hooks, at the 'free' end, and, possibly, other hooks along its length.

Once the fishing weight has settled on the sea-bed, the trace should flow out down tide, with the baited hook free to move in the current, attracting the fish in the process. When the bite comes, the reel line can be run through the loop or loops of the boom,

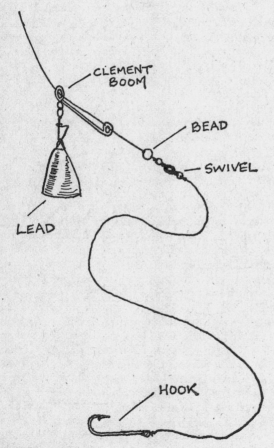

figure 22 Flowing trace

figure 23 Tucked half blood knot

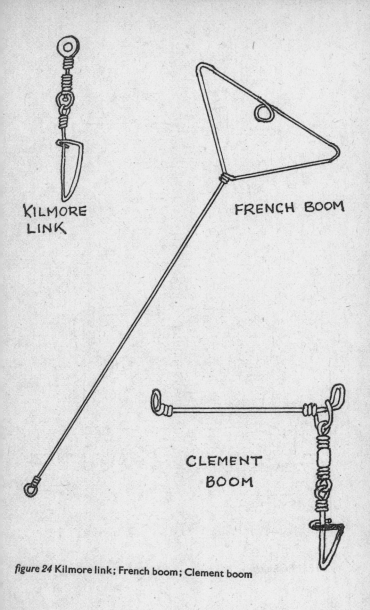

KILMORE
LINK

FRENCH BOOM

CLEMENT
BOOM

figure 24 Kilmore link; French boom; Clement boom

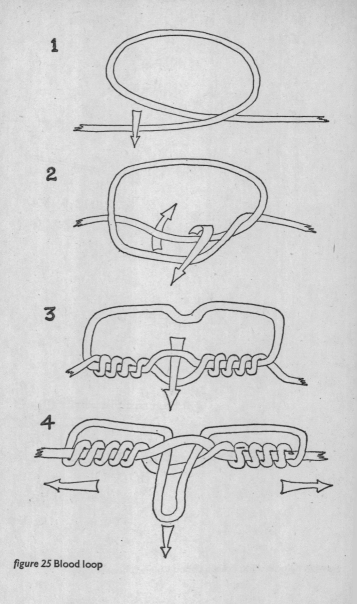

figure 25 Blood loop

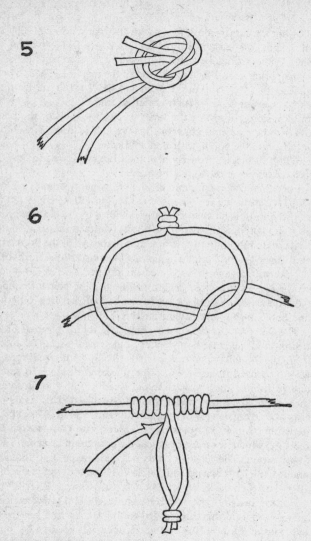

figure 26 To join two ends using blood loop

allowing the fish to move away with the bait without feeling the full weight and resistance of the lead. In weedy fishing conditions, when fishing from a boat, the lead (weight) should be attached to a 'link spring swivel' tied to the end of the reel line. Then, by calculating the 'top level' of the weed bed, say 2 ft (60 cm) from the lead, for example, a 'French boom' should be looped on to the line, by simply inserting the line through the loop of the boom and turning it around, three or four times. The 'trace' is then tied to the end of the boom, with a reliable knot.

With this tackle, properly tied, the trace is allowed to flow out into the tide, over the top of the weed.

For beach-casting, the end tackle is reasonably simple; a 'blood loop' is tied in the reel line, some 12–18 in (30–45 cm) from the end, the loop itself being, ideally, about 4 in (10 cm) long, just long enough, in fact, to take the hook. To attach the hook, simply pass the double end of the loop through the eye of the hook, then over the hook itself, finally tightening the loop around the hook.

Now you have your hook tied on, about 12–18 in (30–45 cm) up the line, with a 'free' length of line trailing below the hook. Now tie a 'spring-link' swivel to the end of the 'free' length of line, and clip your lead (weight) to this.

This will prove to be a good, simple rig for all types of beach-casting and general shore fishing, but, when you need to cast from the beach under particularly strong tidal conditions, or when you need to achieve maximum casting distance to reach a known fishing 'mark', or to avoid weed or other obstructions, then a special casting 'leader' should be utilized. This leader consists of a strong length of line, usually about 30 lb (14 kg) breaking strain, which is tied, with an appropriate knot, to the finer reel line, which, for most practical purposes, will be around 18 lb (8 kg) strain. The length of this heavier 'leader' line should be about the length of two rods; that is, if the rod you are using is 10 ft (3 m) then the leader will be 20 ft (6 m) long.

For this heavier type of beach-casting, the end tackle is tied on as before but, in this case, is tied to the 'leader' and not the reel line. Naturally, both the reel and leader will need to be joined, again with an appropriate knot. In practice, this 'leader' tackle is

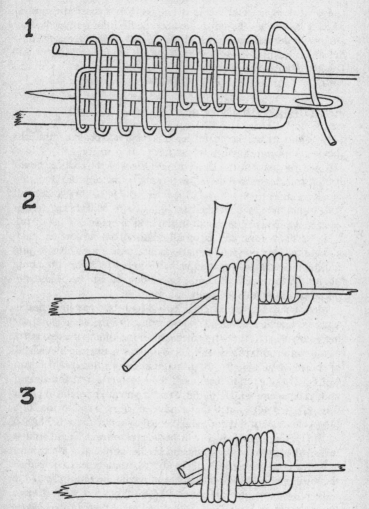

figure 27 Leader knot

reeled in until the end tackle is hanging from the rod-tip, and when it is cast, all the impact is absorbed by the heavier leader and not to the reel line, which would surely break under such conditions. Incidentally, the best knot for joining the two lengths of line is the simple blood knot.

Boat-fishing and beach-casting tackle

Now to end tackles for boat fishing. Since this is probably the last tackle the beginner will buy, we have left it to the end of this chapter, for that reason. Everything starts with the rod, for boat-fishing rods are now 'classed' according to the appropriate line-breaking strain for each rod. So, when you go to buy your boat rod, it will usually be classed as 20 lb, 30 lb, 50 lb (9 kg, 14 kg, 23 kg), etc. The average boat-fishing rod is between 6 ft (1.8 m) and 7 ft (2 m) long and is usually made from hollow or solid glass-fibre. Our previous remarks concerning rings, fittings and finish on beach-casting rods will still apply to boat rods, but, obviously, the length of handle on a boat rod will be of less importance, although not exactly unimportant.

Most boat rods are made in two pieces, one rod joint and a separate handle section, so make absolutely sure, when purchasing your rod, that the fitting mechanism for joining the two parts of the rod is both robust and reliable. Always buy the 'line class' of rod most suitable for the fishing conditions under which you will be working; most beginners tend to buy a rod too heavy, and, as a general guide, we think that if you are just starting boat fishing, you will be much better advised to get a rod in the 20 lb (9 kg) class. With this rod, you can safely use a 15 lb (6.5 kg) to 25 lb (11.5 kg) line, which will be adequate for all boat-fishing tasks, other than wreck fishing and similar extra heavy jobs.

As for boat-fishing reels, there are two main types to consider; the multiplier and the centrepin, and, while the multiplier is the most popular reel for all but the 'heavier' types of boat fishing, the centrepin, or 'drum' reel, will come into its own for the heavier jobs – particularly boat fishing for large conger eels and skate.

1

2

3

4

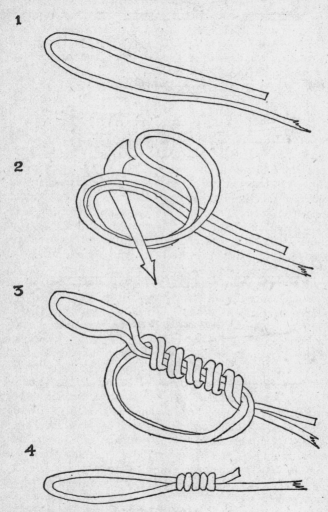

figure 28 A plain loop with five tucks

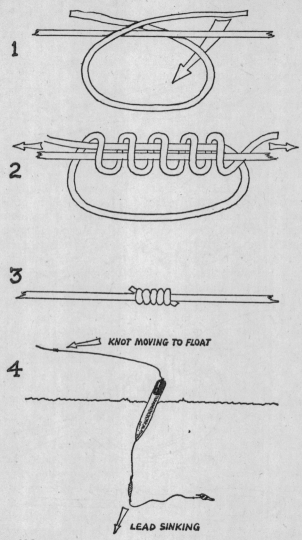

1

2

3

4

KNOT MOVING TO FLOAT

LEAD SINKING

figure 29 Stop knot

The multiplier for boat work is the same, in mechanical principle, as the multiplier used for beach fishing, but the shape is quite different; the spool is much deeper and more narrow, and is usually made from chromed metal.

The reason for this 'chunkier' construction is that the rigours of boat fishing are very hard on the reel, and, if the reel is too weak for the job, the spool can actually burst under the tremendous pressure exerted by the line. So, choose your reel with great care; don't be tempted by very cheap, inferior reels; that will be false economy, as your reel can be aptly described as the 'engine room' of your outfit, and, if that breaks down, you're sunk!

The centrepin reel is much more simple in design and construction, consisting simply of a plastic or metal drum revolving on a stout spindle – with a pair of handles to turn it. A ratchet mechanism is usually provided to control the reel when the angler puts it down in the boat. However, before leaving the centrepins, there is on the market a more sophisticated type, made in Australia, which is fitted with a clutch and non-reverse mechanism similar to a multiplier. These reels are extremely good to use and are available in several sizes. If you can afford one, it will be a good investment.

Although some anglers prefer the centrepin for its simplicity, the most widely used reel for boat fishing is the multiplier. Choose one that will hold enough line – of the correct breaking strain to suit your rod. For a 20 lb (9 kg) rod, 300 yds (275 m) of 20 lb (9 kg) line is ideal, with similar amounts of line for the heavier reels.

Now, for a look at some of the 'odds and ends' of tackle that you will need, beginning with that small, but vital 'link', the swivel. Swivels are used as joining links for traces and the various tackles. The most common type is the 'barrel' swivel, or plain swivel, which varies in size a great deal; so be careful not to get your swivels too large or too small, they could let you down at a vital moment; the most appropriate size, in our view, for normal fishing under general conditions, is about size 1/0.

Leads (weights) can be linked to a 'spring link' swivel, and, as a good guide, remember that the larger the lead being used, the larger will be the swivel required.

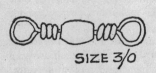

SIZE 3/0

SPRING
LINK
SWIVEL

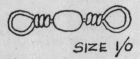

SIZE 1/0

SIZE 2

SNAP
SWIVEL

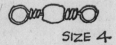

SIZE 4

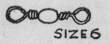

SIZE 6

PLAIN SWIVELS

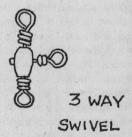

3 WAY
SWIVEL

figure 30 Swivels

For beach-casting, think in terms of hook sizes 4 to 2/0, with leads ranging from 2 oz (57 g) to 8 oz (227 g).

Another widely used piece of end tackle is the 'sliding boom' which is a device designed to keep the hook, or hooks, free of the line when casting and fishing. There are many different shapes and sizes available, so choose wisely – and avoid any that are fitted with extra 'gadgets'; these, in our experience, are an unnecessary encumbrance. Always keep your terminal tackle simple; the less fussy and complicated they are, the less chance you have of snags and tangles – in and out of the water.

Wire booms, again, are found in many different shapes and sizes, and of these, the 'French' boom is by far the easiest to attach or remove from the tackle, without the necessity for knots or links. So, always keep a few in your tackle box: they're fairly cheap and very handy.

Beads are used as stops for sliding booms, and are threaded on to the line above the stop swivel. Some anglers insist on using red or white beads, believing that they help to attract the fish to the bait.

An essential item of tackle, when after the 'sharp teeth' fish such as tope, conger, large skate, etc., is the wire trace. In recent years, important advances have been made in their design and manufacture, and they are now available in multi-strand stainless steel, covered with nylon, in a range of many different breaking strains. Always choose a wire trace that is a little heavier than your reel line to begin with, as those teeth we have just mentioned are very powerful, and your tackle needs all the protection it can get. Remember, also, that a fish's teeth can inflict very nasty wounds, so have a healthy respect for them – and when landing them, don't attempt to remove the hook until the fish is either dead, or under control – and then, only tackle the job with a good pair of pliers.

Two more essential items for the serious sea angler's kit; a good, strong, sharp knife and a pair of reliable pliers. The knife is for cutting up bait, nylon line etc. (but never wire), and is very useful for preparing the catch of fish ready to take home for the pot. The pliers will cut wire, remove hooks from fish (and

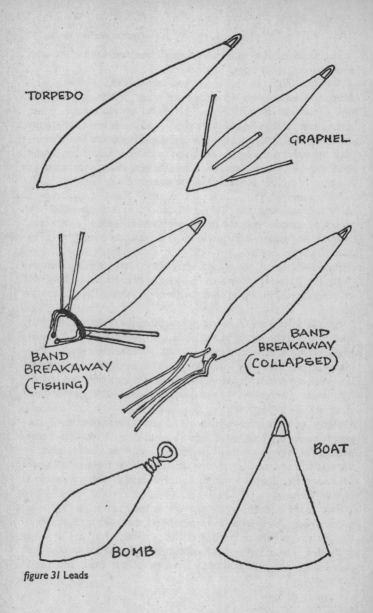

TORPEDO

GRAPNEL

BAND
BREAKAWAY
(FISHING)

BAND
BREAKAWAY
(COLLAPSED)

BOMB

BOAT

figure 31 Leads

trousers!) and will come in handy for all sorts of minor repair jobs to reels.

You will also need what is known as a 'gaff' – a large metal hook for landing fish. You can buy a gaff head in your tackle shop, then simply lash it to an ash wood broom handle, finally giving the wood some good coats of waterproof varnish and binding the handle with a good 'non-slip' material like heavy twine or fine rope. For boat fishing, the gaff handle can be shorter. The point of your gaff should always be kept sharp and clean, and for safety's sake, cover it with some stout rubber tubing when it's not in use.

Sea angling weights, or leads, both for beach-casting and boat fishing, come in a wide variety of shapes and sizes, and, unless you intend fishing in one place only, where the depth and speed of the tide is constant, you will need a good range in your box. For beach-casting, there are two basic types in general use, the 'torpedo' lead, which – would you believe! – is slim and pointed like a torpedo and designed to shoot through the air with the minimum resistance. The other one, the 'grapnel' lead, has four wires moulded into the forward end, and these dig into the sea-bed, to hold the tackle against the tide. These good leads allow the angler to fish comfortably in tidal conditions that would prove to be too strong for un-wired leads. Very often, when you're fishing with a torpedo – or other smooth lead – and the tide or current gets too strong, a quick change over to a 4 oz (113 g) grapnel lead will do the trick.

Another type of lead, a little more intricate, but extremely useful, has appeared on tackle shop shelves during the last few years; this is the 'breakaway' lead, and here's how it works. It is similar, in basic design, to the grapnel lead, but the built-in wires are designed to collapse inwards and fold away, when pressure is applied to the lead. So, whereas the grapnel lead, with its fixed wires, will often snag on underwater obstructions when being wound in by the angler, the breakaway lead folds in its wires and is much more easily retrieved.

In fact, there are two types of breakaway grapnel leads on the market: the 'bead' breakaway, which has four beads lodging in sockets in the lead, to keep the wires in the outer 'fishing' position; and the 'band' breakaway lead, which, instead of beads, has a rubber band for the same purpose. Of the two, and having tested both thoroughly, we prefer the 'band', and certainly both the 'bead' and the 'band' are improvements on the conventional grapnel lead, especially when fishing very snaggy sea-beds.

Leads for boat fishing are, by comparison with beach-casting leads, a much more simple proposition, and the commonest type is the conical boat lead. This is usually available from 12 oz (340 g) to 32 oz (900 g) and above, so choose the ones most suited to your tidal fishing conditions. Other shapes include the 'grip' leads and, just to bewilder the beginner, there are various other varieties in the tackle shops; but, if you take our advice, you'll stick with the good old-fashioned conical leads – and find them very efficient.

Your leads are best carried in a stout canvas bag, preferably made with a tie-cord at its mouth; also, whoever makes it should double-sew the seams or you might have a very painful experience – when a heavy lead escapes through the seam and drops on your toe! Keep two bags, one for beach leads, the other for boat leads, and mark them well; don't travel miles to do some beach fishing only to find a bag of boat leads – and nothing else.

The general question of tackle-carrying gear is an important one. Tackle bags should always be strong and waterproof, and, take a tip from us and have two bags – one for tackle, bait, etc., and another for food. Lugworm sandwiches don't make a very pleasant meal!

For beach fishing, you will need a rod-rest to prop your rod upon after you have cast out the tackle and are waiting for a bite. These fall into two categories: the spiked type for sand or gravel beaches, or the tripod type, standing on three legs and particularly useful for harder types of terrain.

You can easily make your own spiked rod-rest from a broom-handle, sharpening the lower end to a point and fitting it with an angling umbrella spike which your friendly tackle dealer will provide. This should be glued into position with strong, waterproof adhesive, as it will have to contend with some strong treat-

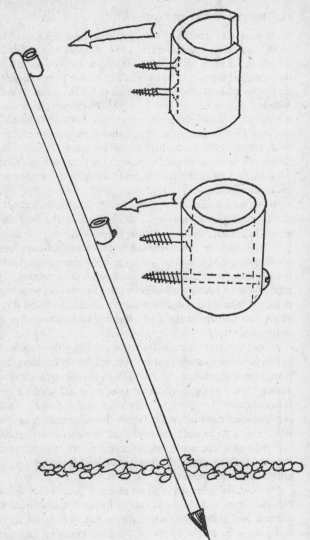

figure 32 Beach rod-rest

ment over the seasons. Then, get some 1½ in (3.8 cm) diameter black polythene tubing and cut two pieces from the end about 2 in (5 cm) deep. Cut one of these on the section, so that roughly two-thirds of the 'circle' remains, then screw it firmly to the broomstick about 2 in (5 cm) from the top, using two small brass screws (counter-sunk), one above the other, in the centre of the 'U' of tubing. The other (whole) section of tubing should then be screwed into position, in line with the first section, but about 15 in (38 cm) below the top of the broomstick. In this section, however, the lower screw (nearest to the bottom spike) should be long enough to pass through both walls of the tubing and into the broomstick.

In practice, the spike is pushed into the beach, right down to the bottom plastic tubing bracket, so that the bottom (long) screw is actually resting on the ground. When you have made your cast, jam the bottom of the rod into the bottom tube, where it will come to rest against the long screw, then push the rod into the open (top) section of tube, where it will be retained comfortably without causing abrasion to the varnish on your rod. This makes a simple but effective beach rod-rest, and you'll find that when you want to strike a bite the rod will come out of the rest quite smoothly.

A beach tripod rest can easily be made by the angler. Simply get three stout 'garden' canes, about 5 ft (1.5 m) long, and lash them together about 4 in (10 cm) from the top, using a good strong cord for the purpose. Again, a liberal coating of waterproof varnish, particularly on the cord, will prolong the life of the rest and keep out salt water. To use this rest, place it on the beach with one 'leg' pointing seawards and the other two splayed well out, then cast, and place the beach rod on the 'tripod', just above the cord lashing. And, just like the other rod-rest, give it plenty of good varnish for protection.

Many sea anglers like fishing at night, and it is a well-known fact that some fish, like cod, for example, are nocturnal feeders, moving well inshore to feed, after dark. Offshore fishing, from a boat, can also be productive during the hours of darkness, but, whatever you do, always go with an experienced local boatman

- and observe the sea-fishing safety rules that are detailed later in this book. For any type of serious night fishing, you will require a good light, and a robust portable electric 'lantern', battery operated, and preferably one of those with a 'swivelling' beam, will be excellent. Apart from this 'adjustable' light, however, you will also need a good 'background' light, to illuminate your bait box, for example, or tied to the top of the cabin, if you are fishing from a boat.

One of the paraffin pressure lamps or gas cartridge types will be ideal, but both types are dangerous if they are not handled with care, and can get knocked or kicked over, with disastrous consequences. Be ultra careful with all types of 'flame' lamps.

Assuming that you have caught a lot of good fish, you will need a bag in which to carry them home (you will, of course, only take the ones you need for 'the pot', and return small or unwanted ones to the sea). The best type of fish bag is one made from sacking or matting; it tends to 'breathe' better and keeps the fish nice and fresh. Unfortunately, it also has a nasty habit of leaking fishy, salty moisture all over the place, so we will recommend a good plastic bag, but not too 'thin', as some fish have sharp spines which can puncture the plastic; also, as these polythene types of bags make the fish 'sweat', you are advised to chop off the heads of the fish and roughly 'gut' them, finally washing the gutted fish well in sea water before popping them into the bag. They should travel quite well in the bag, providing that the journey is not too long and the weather not too hot. The final tidying up and filleting, ready for the pot, will best be left to wives or mums, when you get home.

Our final word on sea fishing tackle concerns its care. Like most things today, it is expensive, so take good care of it; neglected or badly worn tackle is inefficient, and the weakened rod, blunt hook or frayed line has lost many good specimen fish. Losing a fish in this way is not 'bad luck' - it is simply bad management.

Never overload yourself with tackle when you go fishing; it is a great temptation for many beginners to take with them more tackle than they will ever need for a day's fishing; a couple of good rods and reels, plus the rest of the vital bits and pieces, will be ample. Anyone who has been in the Boy Scouts, or the Forces, will know that whatever baggage you start off with becomes progressively heavier at every few yards!

As for sea fishing clothing, always take plenty of good, warm clobber with you, with a heavy preference for woollens. Even in summertime, the seashore can be cold and damp, and this applies even more strongly to boat fishing offshore. In our experience, the best type of fishing clothing consists of woollen sweaters, 'topped off' with a good waterproof jacket and trousers.

Finally, make sure that you have an adequate first-aid kit with you, at all times. Accidents *do* occur, when least expected, and for minor injuries, a little immediate attention can save hospitalization later. When you go boat fishing, there are several very important articles of kit that *must* be in the boat before you leave the shore or jetty. These are the lifejacket, pocket compass, distress flares and, of course, the first-aid kit. If we have laboured the 'safety' angle throughout this book, we make no apologies; the sea is quite dangerous enough by itself without flying hooks and leads, sharp knives, and inexperienced people in impossibly small boats. So, make us a firm promise – safety first, every time.

5 Sea fishing methods

Casting

In tennis, it is the quality of delivery that gets the ball, successfully, or unsuccessfully, to the required target. It is the same with all sports that deliver a missile to a given target; football, archery, basketball, etc. In sea fishing, the principle is the same; a baited tackle must be delivered, accurately, to a chosen spot. Consequently, it is the perfection of the delivery – in this case, casting – that must be studied. And, as in most fields in which perfection must be achieved, it is the practice that makes perfection. To the beginner, unfamiliar with his tackle, the need for constant practice is essential, but, on the credit side, it is like learning to ride a bicycle, which, once learned, will never be forgotten.

The most common mistake, with beginners to casting, is that they try right from the start to achieve long, difficult casts before they have mastered the 'feel' and technicalities of their tackle. Don't do this: start gently, you're not out to break the hundred-yard casting barrier at the first attempt – you'd be foolish to try. No, get to know the rod and reel – and practise, time and time again, gradually building up your competence and confidence; twenty-five yards – fifty – then, perhaps the hundred, or more.

To begin with, let's imagine we're starting to learn with a simple beach-casting rod and multiplier reel, complete with lead. At this stage, it will be advisable to dispense with the hooks, for obvious reasons. Now, you're all tackled up, with a lead fixed to the end of the line. Hold the rod, horizontally, at shoulder height, and reel in the line until the lead is just clear of the ground, say about 3–4 ft (90–120 cm) from the top rod-ring. If you are right-handed, place the right hand below the reel and put your thumb firmly on the spool; then, with the left hand, release the 'free spool' lever to disengage the spool from the driving gear. The left hand should then be placed upon the butt of the rod. Now, with the reel below the rod and the rod held comfortably at shoulder height, move into a casting position, placing the outside of the left foot in the direction you wish to cast. The feet should be spread comfortably apart. During this manoeuvre, *don't*, whatever you do, relax the pressure on your right thumb (the one controlling the spool) or a bird's nest will result. Now you are ready to begin the cast, for the first time.

Holding the rod, 'rock' the lead gently by shifting your body weight from foot to foot, keeping the rod in the same body position. As you 'rock' the lead, it will swing towards the butt of the rod, then away again, beyond the tip of the rod. When the lead reaches the top of its swing towards you, and is close under the rod, begin the cast. Here's how.

Smoothly force the right hand upwards, pulling down on the left hand at the same time, and half turning the body as you do so, bringing your back muscles into play to aid the cast. As the lead is cast forwards and upwards, release your thumb from the spool, and, as the lead gathers speed through the air, gently 'brush' the thumb against the spool (not the line) to control the cast. Once the lead has 'hit ground', the thumb can be placed firmly on the spool again and at the same time the free spool lever can be disengaged. Learn to cast like this, and drastic 'bird's nests' will be avoided.

Now, what have you achieved? A good cast of some 25 to 30 yds (20 to 27 m), no bird's nests, and an urgent desire to get an even better, longer cast. Good, so try it again, with just a little more effort behind the cast; a smooth, non-jerking action, that, with a little more practice, will put you among the best. After a few casts like this, you will discover an interesting point. As your 'smoothness' of casting improves, you will find that less 'thumbing' of the spool will be required. In point of fact, this thumbing action is only really necessary when the reel's delivery of line is faster than the speed of the outgoing, slowing down, lead. The crucial point usually occurs when the lead is still climbing – and beginning to slow down against gravity and air pressure – just before reaching the highest point of the cast. Once over the top of its zenith, the lead will start to speed up again as it plummets downwards. It's all a bit highly technical, we know, but bear with us, go through the motions, as we have described them, carefully and persistently, and you'll soon get the hang of it.

But, if you're going to practise casting somewhere other than in the sea, or a big lake, maybe even in a park or a large garden, do be extra careful; a 4 oz (113 g) lead gets up quite a speed during a good cast, so make sure that all the kids and pets are locked indoors, and there is a marked absence of plate glass in the near vicinity.

Sometimes, when learning to cast, the lead will 'break off' in flight, and this is usually caused by a sudden 'bird's nest', or an over-enthusiastic jerk at some point during the start of the cast. As previously said, a lead travelling at maximum speed is easily capable of snapping a quite heavy line if it comes to a sudden stop. So, be careful. A break-off lead can quite easily travel *at least* 400 yds (360 m) between you and the nearest obstruction, and, as a missile, would be very lethal. So, take our advice, allow at least 200 yds (180 m) in front and behind you, when practising.

Once you have mastered this simple overhead cast, and can cast reasonable distances without serious problems, then you can improve your technique – and fishing efficiency – by trying the 'lay back' style of casting. Start by placing your feet slightly further apart than you would for the overhead cast, allowing most of the weight to be taken by the back foot. Then, leaning the body backwards over the rear foot, until the front foot has little or no weight upon it and is acting as a 'counterweight', begin the cast, using the same overhead style as before, so that the whole weight of the body is shifted, dramatically, until the lead is released, and all the body weight is over the front foot. The advantage of this cast is that *all* the body's power is utilized, usually in a more powerful, longer cast.

Other, more difficult methods of casting can be tried and perfected, at a later stage, but, in the main, the two basic methods we have described are both simple and effective for most types of fishing the beginner will be likely to encounter.

Casting with the 'fixed spool' reel, as distinct from the multiplier, is similar in all respects, except for the handling of the reel. To cast, begin as before, but open the 'bale arm' on the reel, putting the line into its 'free' position. As you cast, the line can be controlled by hooking the index finger around it, releasing the finger as you need the line to travel out. When using something like a 6 oz (170 g) lead (or bigger) with the fixed spool reel, you could find difficulty in controlling the weight and power of the lead with the index finger, because of the extra power on the line. Well, here's a good tip. Take a turn of the line around the rod-handle and place the thumb upon it, then pull back the bale arm. This will allow the thumb to trap the line firmly, until you need to release it.

Once the cast is made, your worries are over, for a turn of the reel handle will automatically close the bale arm, to control the line once the lead has 'grounded'. Usually, the multiplier will be capable of longer casts than the fixed spool, but, for general purposes, you will not need to cast 100 yds (90 m) every cast; but the occasion could arise when the very long cast could mean the difference between a good catch and a 'blank' day; so try to perfect the use of both reels, if you can.

Remember that size and strength of the individual is not a good key to successful casting. Many of the more successful competition surf-casters are smallish men, but men who have, through sheer hard work and practice, perfected their *technique*.

This 'thumbing' of the multiplier reel is an art which will, in all probability, take you some time to learn, and, we regret to forecast, will cause you some unholy 'bird's nests' and a lot of frustration. But stick with it – you'll come through, we know. If it gets you down, however, there is a device on the market now called an 'Anti-Lash', which is designed to fit on to the better classes of multiplier reels; it is excellent and well worth the money asked. Similarly, some multipliers have built-in 'thumbing' devices, but, in our experience, unlike the 'Anti-Lash', tend to slow down the whole cast, with an inevitable reduction in distance. Without doubt, the ultimate 'tool' for efficient distance casting is a multiplier with a good, free-running spool, and completely devoid of devices and gadgets.

Shore fishing

The average beginner to sea fishing, once he has mastered some reasonable degree of casting, usually trots off to the nearest pier or jetty, and believing that there is some safety in numbers, joins a host of other fishermen, themselves in various stages of competence, and immediately enters a rather frightening world of elbow-to-elbow jostling for fishing space, flying lines, hooks and leads – and not a small degree of bad temper and language.

Don't, we beg of you, start at such a place; unless, of course, you are lucky to reside at a particularly remote, uncrowded part of the coast where you have a wide choice of untenanted harbour wall, piers, breakwaters and jetties. No, the open beach is the place for you to start, so let's take a good close look at beach fishing, and how to pick yourself a good spot.

For many beach anglers, the one basic recommendation of a good spot is its nearness to a good, convenient car-parking area. Well, you'll leave such spots to the idle, unless you *know* that good fish are to be taken there. We have found, on many occasions, that a nice walk through the fields to the cliff-top, a smart scramble down a rough path to the bottom, then a three-quarter-mile stroll to a little-known 'hot spot' along a boulder-strewn beach, will serve for better fishing – and a quieter, more attractive environment; all right, it's not particularly *convenient*, and you burned up quite a few calories getting there, but, oh boy, the fishing! Of course, now that good secluded fishing gets harder to find every year, this type of fishing spot will be the exception to the rule, but, remember what we have said; to find a spot that has never been fished by anyone else should reap dividends, for usually, the further you get 'off the beaten track', the better the fishing should be.

Let's take a look at a typical stretch of open shingle beach on the east coast of England. Most anglers tend to park the car at the end of the approach road, walk up over the shingle bank and start fishing, only walking far enough to meet a reasonably vacant area of beach. You won't do it that way. About 400 yards (360 m) south along the beach, and easily seen by the intelligent angler, there is a natural depression where the shingle bank is several feet lower than anywhere else. Here, the water will be deeper, making long casts unnecessary. There are other signs to look for, too. Any natural or man-made obstruction like a groyne, jetty, sea defence, rock outcrop, or kelp bed will provide good 'cover' and feeding grounds for sea fish; so, where you discover an obstruction like this, have a good look at it, during low water, and fish it as the tide rises, casting into the clear water at either side.

Where the bottom is sandy, you might discover 'channels' in the sand where the tide will begin to run in as it flows on the flood. It is in these channels normally you will first find your fish, species like flounders and dabs, often swimming up in only a few inches of water, finding some protection from the 'predatory' fish, like bass, in the darker 'colour' of the water as it mixes with the sand and other substances on the flood. The bass, too, will follow the flood tide, up the channels and beaches, to feed upon the smaller fish and other creatures, and, very often, will be seen swirling and rippling the surface of the water as they forage for food.

River estuaries, although not strictly regarded as 'beach' fishing spots, frequently provide excellent fishing marks, but, for the beginner, the tidal flow in such places is often heavy, making the pursuit of 'sensitive' fishing very difficult.

Those anglers who live by the sea, or very close to it, are in luck; they will soon be able to familiarize themselves with the local terrain, spending hours at low water, walking the foreshore and studying, at great length, the special characteristics of the bottom and storing away, in their minds, all the likely places to fish.

If, however, you live a long way from the sea, then your fishing and territorial information will take longer to acquire. But your friendly tackle dealer, even an inland one, will usually help you; even if he doesn't know the particular stretch you are going to himself, one of his customers might be able to give you a few useful tips about the best 'spots'. In the main, anglers *are* friendly, helpful people, and in most busy tackle shops, simply drop the word that you're a beginner, going fishing in an unfamiliar place, and you'll be pleasantly surprised by their keenness to help. In the same way, the angling club is a great source of help and companionship for the beginner. Most coastal towns have at least one, and you'll probably be welcomed with open arms and showered with advice – but, be careful, for, with great respect, it will not all be good advice!

However, whether the advice is sound or not, most sea anglers are the 'salt of the earth', always at hand to lend you bait, clothing, food and, above all, advice. Take it all in good heart, and, as you progress, sort out the good from the bad, until you are able to go off, on your own, to some nice quiet stretch of beach and 'do your own thing'.

Let's assume that you've done just that, and you are now ensconced on your bit of beach, ready to fish. Your tackle is all made up, the hook, or hooks, are baited and you are ready for the first cast. Firstly, find out which way the tide is running and cast out, slightly *uptide*. As your lead weight settles on the bottom, after the cast, tighten the line by reeling in a little, and wait for the lead to settle. It will probably bump around for a moment or two, giving little 'knocks' on the rod top, finally settling on the bottom – then you're fishing.

Mind you, it might not happen like that. If, for example, the lead keeps moving after you have cast, with the line washing further and further downtide, then reel in, put on a slightly heavier lead – or a spiked lead, to hold the bottom – and recast.

On certain days, you might find several changes of lead necessary, until you've found the one to suit the particular tidal conditions at the time. Sometimes, you could even find quite heavy rollers breaking on the shore, and, in these conditions, a lead that is too light will actually be 'thrown' up, bringing it closer to the beach. At times like these, the heavy 'grapnel' leads, as we have described them in the previous chapter, will be the order of the day. At other times, weed can be a big problem when fishing from the beach, especially after a strong gale when masses of thick seaweed have been forced into the shore. Under such conditions, we advise you to use either a plain 'torpedo' lead, which acts as a good weed 'collector', or, better still, the 'breakaway' lead which is invaluable when heavy weed is around.

But, assuming that conditions are reasonably normal, and you have cast out the baited tackle, how do you now recognize a bite, when it comes? Watch your rod-top. There will always be some continual movement on the top of the rod, as you are fishing, but until you get a bite, it will normally take the form of slow, rhythmic 'dipping' as the waves, rolling inshore, give movement to the line and tackle. The bites themselves will usually take two distinct forms; one that pulls the rod-top down in a series of small jerks – or even a strong 'plunge'. This type of bite is caused by the fish actually pulling on the line. The other type of bite is a 'slack line' one, which happens as a fish pulls the end tackle *towards* the shore, making a fairly sudden slack 'bow' in the line between the rod-top and the water. This slackening of the line will be the only indication that the bait has been taken by a fish.

Now for striking at a bite. Striking is the action of pulling the point of the hook into a biting fish, and, to strike effectively, the rod must be swept sharply backwards, over your head, to set the hook. Don't strike while the line is still slack, but reel in line, at the same time taking a couple of steps backwards, away from the water, to speed up the process. Once the line is tight to the rod-top, strike. Smashing the line upwards, like a whiplash, will probably result in a break certainly in the line, even in the rod. On the other hand, a gentle, timid lifting of the rod will not be effective, either. No, take the middle road and give a firm, swift upward strike – that will do the trick.

The 'tight line' bites are more easily dealt with, but, for the beginner, the biggest problem is knowing precisely *when* to strike. The most difficult tight line bite is, without doubt, the sudden plunge, which is often not repeated after the first bite so that the angler has little time to act – and doesn't get a second chance. That beautiful, hard-fighting fish, the bass, is often the culprit with this type of bite. Normally, the average bite will develop gradually, starting with a few tremors on the rod-top, which can be safely ignored, at first. The next indication of the developing bite will be a few short, sharp jerks, finishing with a good firm pull on the top of the rod. When this happens – strike!

Unfortunately, there is no firm 'blueprint' for bites, and, on occasions, you won't get clearly defined, determined bites at all, simply some tremors on the rod-top, which will not, even after some considerable time, develop into anything more positive. When this happens, you should strike at the slightest 'twitch'.

Another thing. The 'quality' of the bite, in terms of strength, will not necessarily determine the size of the fish; very often, the smallest, most timid bite will result in the capture of a big fish, and, in the same way, a very pronounced bite could produce small fish well under a pound in weight. So, be attentive and concentrate on that vital rod-tip. Many beach fishermen will hold the rod all the time they are fishing, to make sure that no bites are missed. This is a good habit to acquire, particularly when fishing in calm conditions. But, because holding a fairly heavy sea rod, for long periods at a time, can be fatiguing, most anglers will employ some sort of rod rest, even if it is used only for resting the rod while 'baiting up' the tackle.

If you use a rod rest, please don't get into the habit of casting out, then wandering down the beach for a chat with your fellow anglers, for so often it is at that precise moment the fish will bite. Fish are very unobliging in this respect, and you'll often find that it is just during that moment of inattention that things happen; taking a cup of hot soup from the flask, for example, or answering an urgent call of nature! It is almost as though the fish know, the cunning blighters!

Now back to the fishing. You've had a good bite, struck with some success and the fish is on. Now you have the pleasant, long-awaited task of 'playing' the fish and bringing it out of the deeper water into the shallows, where you can handle it. The main thing to remember, when playing a fish, is – and this is vitally important – *keep a tight line*. But, and here's the secret, don't be too forceful; the line, your rod – and the fish's mouth – can stand so much pressure, after which, bingo! everything is lost. This fish-playing is rather like handling a horse (perhaps even a woman!): it is just that sophisticated degree of gentleness, that makes the day.

For heaven's sake, don't reel in furiously when playing a fish. Use some care and thought, keeping a steady, tight rein on your quarry, all the time. It is just this continual pressure that tires your fish, gradually wearing him down, until the time when he is ready to be drawn into the shallows. The worst possible fault in beach fishing is to haul a hooked fish into shallow water while it is still 'fresh', with plenty of fight left in it. The inevitable conclusion is having to deal with a sprightly fish, on a tight line, among heavy breakers, with the result that lines – and tempers – get very frayed. No, tire your fish, gradually, while it is still in deepish water, finally bringing it in, tired and submissive, to the shallows, where it can be picked up with ease, with no danger of a sudden lunge for freedom – and a broken line.

There are various ways of 'beaching' a fish, according to sea conditions at the time. By far the best method, when possible, is to draw the fish gently up into very shallow water at the edge of the beach, then pick it up. But when very heavy seas are running and big waves abound on the shore, you should draw your fish right up on to a dry bit of beach, to avoid the troublesome waves as you unhook it. We've seen it, several times – a beginner grappling with a fish, buffeted by waves, and finally slithering down on his knees, only to be dragged into the water by the undertow of a big wave.

You can, of course, use a net or a gaff, when fishing off the beach, but usually, this method applies to larger, or more dangerous fish, where handling is hazardous. You'll find, at your first attempt, that picking up a fish, fresh from the water, can be a slippery business. Take a tip from us and always carry a mesh onion – or carrot – bag, which your friendly greengrocer will supply you with, and wrapping this around the body of the fish, apply a little more pressure than you would with bare hands – and the fish is yours. Fish can escape through slipping through your hands at the waterside, and this is a very frustrating business indeed.

Once you have landed your fish, you'll want to kill it, ready to store away and take home. This can be done, humanely, by delivering several sharp, heavy blows on the head, above and slightly behind the eyes, using a stone, a pair of heavy pliers (which you have used for unhooking) or some other 'blunt instrument' designed for the purpose. Please, do not let your fish die, slowly, on the beach – or anywhere else, come to that; it just causes unnecessary suffering – for which you might possibly be repaid in some 'afterlife'. Any undersized or similarly unwanted fish, not required for the pot or for bait, should be unhooked gently, and returned, also gently, to its natural environment; you'll be a much better person for this.

Another thing to watch, vigilantly, when beach fishing, is the peculiarities of tides. As the tide moves in, so should you, drawing back your tackle as the tide rises up the shore. On occasions, the odd, large wave will surprise you, by crashing on to the beach, further up than the others. If this happens, and you're not ready for it, your tackle, bait, lamps and anything else can be gone in a flash, leaving you that much poorer – and wetter. So, when the tide is on the move up the beach, move back with it, giving yourself plenty of time.

Beach fishing at night can be a very rewarding method of fishing, but, to give yourself a better chance, try to select a rising tide, just after dark. Casting at night can be more difficult than in daylight, as you can't easily see the flight of the lead; but, make no mistake, once you have mastered the difficulties, you will be well compensated, for, in our view, beach fishing is normally at its best when everyone else has gone to bed.

For night fishing, you'll need a good light, and we have found that the best thing for the job is a 'headlight' lamp strapped to the forehead, which leaves your hands free for the task in hand; baiting-up, casting and striking, etc. An additional lamp near the bait box will be a good idea, too, if only to pinpoint its location, as you move around. When using lights of any type on the beach, don't flash them, unnecessarily, to seaward – any more than you can help, that is, or you'll find the local coastguards getting a bit edgy – with good reason. It tends to waste your batteries as well.

To really get the flavour of beach fishing, try a little cooking. Yes – cooking! Some of our most poignant memories of the beach involve aromatic driftwood fires, with steaming saucepans of hot soup atop of them. In the same vein, a good coke 'brazier' fire will do wonders for cold hands and feet on a chill night on the foreshore. Other anglers tend to get drawn towards a beach fire; and a sociable chat, sharing a hot cup of cocoa, with complete strangers, makes for a memorable occasion, particularly when the fishing is 'quiet'. But, be warned, don't prolong your chats, it is at such times that the bite of the night will come – and you not ready for it!

Fishing from piers, breakwaters, jetties and rocks

Unlike fishing from a flat, even a shelving, beach, fishing from a solid vantage point – like a pier or breakwater, for example, some distance *above* the water – produces several important problems, not the least of which are difficulties in controlling lines, landing fish and, above all, the general safety of life and limb. Most piers have safety rails to protect the angler, but it is not so with working harbours, sea walls and natural outcrops of rock. Therefore, when fishing from such places, extra care must be taken. Don't get too close to the edge, that's the main warning; there will probably be deep water below you, turbulent or strong current water, at that. Also, such places can often be slippery with wet weed or algae, so watch your step. Remember, too, that the large, unplanned wave can literally wash you off such places, and the very least that could happen would be a severe wetting. Recently, we heard of two anglers who were drowned after being washed off a harbour wall into a rough sea. Think about that when you go to these places.

The sea, as we have explained, is extremely unpredictable, and the 'freak' wave, even in calm weather conditions, can – and does – happen, catching the angler off his guard. Waves, generally, will reach up higher as the tide floods, adding several feet to the wave's 'range'. Watch it.

Piers and harbour walls offer the easiest vantage points for the sea angler, and, for the beginner, are good for a number of reasons. The obvious reason is that they give you ready access to deeper water, making very long casts unnecessary. In these conditions, the very worst 'caster' still has a good chance of getting fish. Another, less obvious, benefit is that these fishing places, especially in the more popular resorts, will usually be peopled by other anglers, many of them highly experienced men, who will be glad to offer help and advice at a moment's notice. Here, you can also watch, at close range, other anglers casting, catching and playing fish, using the drop-net and various other aids and arts of the pier angler. Mind you, bear in mind that you are just as likely to see how *not* to do it, and you're bound to spot obvious errors in tackle and techniques, learning from these mistakes, yourself. It's all good fun – and highly instructional, one way or the other.

The local pier is a great place to find the 'Local Expert', much respected, admired and sometimes secretly envied by the others. Study him well, notice how easily and quickly he handles his gear, baits his hook and makes smooth, effortless casts. Notice, too, the avid concentration with which he studies his rod-tip – and how fast he moves when that first faint tremor signals the developing bite. His eventual strike will be swift and professional, and, with little or no fuss, the fish will be eased, gently, into the drop-net, which will probably be lowered for him by another angler – one he can trust. Once on the deck, the fish will get a sharp, unemotional tap on the head and will then be stowed away in the fishbag – probably among several of its fellows. Another smooth cast will follow, and the process repeated.

Watch the Local Expert, closely. Take time off from your own fishing if necessary and try to emulate his admirable economy of effort and smooth, practised skill. We are the first to aver that fishing cannot be learned entirely from books. A few hours spent studying a real 'master' will complement all that you have read and heard, helping you to become the Local Expert of the future.

Quite the reverse type of angler, encountered all too often, is the 'Pier Menace', with his characteristic heavy line and light leads. His tackle will be drifting, constantly, into everyone else's on the pier, always supposing that he hasn't cast it there in the first place! The worst breed of Pier Menace is the noisy one, with his continual boasting, complaining and commenting. Noisy Menace will 'borrow' bait, leads, swivels, hooks – and anything else he can lay his fatuous hands on, anything from an aspirin to a cup of soup. Avoid him like the plague – and do, please, try not to develop into one yourself, not even a little one. We're sure you won't.

Now for the basic skills required to fish, successfully, from piers, walls or rocks. Those piers that are supported by 'legs', allowing the tide to pass underneath, are usually built straight out from the shore, and *across* the flow of the tide, which means that, when you cast, you cast up into flowing tide or down tide as it flows away from the pier. Solid piers, harbour walls or jetties are usually of very solid construction, acting as a barrier to the tide and forcing it around the outward end, so causing the direction and force of the tide to change. Your first task is to find a suitable fishing spot – from a *tidal* point of view, that is, not from requirements of personal comfort. A common mistake is to select your spot for its convenient proximity to a shelter, seat or snack-bar, and, if this happens to coincide with a good tidal spot, fine, but if it doesn't, move along to a better, albeit a more 'uncomfortable' spot, further down the pier.

For some reason, most pier anglers tend to race for the *end* of the pier or harbour wall, firmly believing that the further out they go, the deeper will be the water – and the bigger the fish. Very often this will be true, but not always. You can discover this factor for yourself, quite easily, by exploring the sea bottom at low tide, looking for deeper gullies closer inshore, or banks of fish-sheltering weeds, rocks, etc. Then, when the tide comes up – and with it the fish – you'll know exactly where to cast your baited line.

During particularly calm weather, it will usually pay to fish the deeper water, but, when the weather is rough, the inshore end of the pier or jetty may provide the best sport, even those parts of the pier which are close to the shore. Try it. Cast just behind the waves as they roll on to the beach, as they churn up the sand or shingle, even small rocks. It is here that you'll probably find your fish, for *they* know that all that movement has exposed their food – the small marine creatures that shelter on the bottom. In the deeper water, safe from such turbulence, their food will be much harder to find.

Now, let's tackle up and start fishing from our pier. For this type of fishing our 'terminal' tackle will be simple, usually a 'flowing trace' made up of a plain barrel swivel, stopping a link swivel that will be clipped to the lead. The trace should be quite short, say between 1 ft (30 cm) and 2 ft (60 cm) long, and will carry only one hook. Now, bait your hook generously – there's no need to skimp on bait – and cast out, up tide. Let the lead settle on the bottom, then tighten up the line. At this stage, you'll notice that the line is entering the water at a steep angle; this is caused by the tide acting on the line, forcing it down, steeply into the water, causing a sharp, tensioned angle from the lead weight on the bottom, up to the rod-top. Bites will usually be indicated by a sudden lift of the rod-top, followed by a slack line, drifting down-tide. When this happens, reel in the slack line, gently, just as you did when fishing from the beach, and once the first contact is felt – strike. Downtide fishing normally produces a 'balloon' of line as the tide flows away from you, and because of this, more lead will be needed than for fishing uptide. Downtide bites will take the form of the traditional jerk-jerk-firm-pull, or even a sudden plunge.

These jerks and plunges, particularly in heavy tides and rough weather, can be quite violent, so, for this type of fishing, your rod will need to be 'anchored' to something solid, while you're waiting for a bite. Several methods can be employed: the rod can be lashed to a pier rail or, if you are fishing from rocks or stone jetties, a cord lanyard can be tied to the butt of the rod, then fixed to something solid – but preferably *not* your tackle box.

If you fish on piers or jetties long enough, one day you're bound to see a rod and reel lost, pulled in either by a fish or, more likely, a piece of flotsam drifting on the tide. Once, we actually saw an angler hook a semi-submerged bale of cotton, and, had he not been very quick to grab his rod, it would have been, almost certainly, hauled over the side. Another chap we know hooked – and landed – a large coal sack. So, don't forget, lots of quite heavy, unexpected things drift around the sea, in the tide, things that will snatch your rod over the edge – watch out for them.

And now to striking. This is a subject that almost warrants a separate book on its own, mainly because bites, of all types, are so unpredictable. As a general rule, don't be tempted to strike at the first tentative tremor but wait for something more positive. If nothing more develops, reel in and check your bait. Do this every time, as the first nibblings could easily have stripped your hook of its bait. However, if the bite does develop, you'll find that the rod-tip will dip, either in one dramatic plunge or in a series of short, sharp jerks. Either way, strike smoothly.

Small fish like whiting, small flatfish, etc., can be hauled up after the very minimum of playing, but bigger fish are excitingly different at the end of a line. They will run and plunge continually, trying to escape the pressure of the hook and line, and here your tackle will be tested to its limits. Finally, you'll have played him out; he's beaten, almost on the surface – but he's still several feet below you. What now?

Well, you have the choice of three actions. If, for example, there is about 6 ft (2 m) between you and the beaten fish, a good, long-handled gaff will get him in, but, remember this – any more than 6 ft (2 m) will mean the employment of the drop-net. If the fish is of a reasonable size, you will need someone to help with the net. While you keep a tight line on your fish, your companion will take the drop-net (which will be of a good size) and manoeuvre it into a position downtide of the fish, which will be, in all probability, lying flapping, feebly, on the surface. Once the net is in position, and sunk just below the surface, you should work your fish (gently) over the mouth of the sunken net. If your pal knows what he is doing, he'll give a quick heave-ho on the net line and, presto! the fish is yours. Whatever you do, don't, at this stage, reel in your line. If you do, and the fish jumps out of the ascending net, your line will almost certainly be snapped like cotton. Forget the line – and the reel; wait until the fish is at your feet before you worry about 'tidying up' your line.

The other method of landing a fish is a 'custom-made' grapnel, best described as a gaff on a string. It contains three barbed points and, in operation, is jerked home, into the fish, again by a companion.

One other method springs to mind and that is 'hand-lining' a fish. This is usually only necessary when you're fishing alone, without a drop-net, gaff or grapnel. There you are, with a good fish beaten and something like 8 ft (2.4 m) between him and you. In a case like this, put down your rod and hand-line the fish up, smoothly and quickly. It's a somewhat 'chancy' method, but often very effective.

Unlike some beaches, most pier and jetty authorities forbid the use of naked lights, including cooking stoves, for obvious reasons. Do familiarize yourself with all the current, local regulations – and don't break the rules; they are there for someone's protection, and if you do go astray angling you could actually be banned from that particular place.

When fishing from rocks, make sure that you have a secure footing and can climb out of the water fairly easily, if you should fall in. Also, see that all your gear is safely and tidily stowed, yet all handy when needed. If you go to an unfamiliar stretch of rocks, you'll need some sort of light to find your way around, but, in a case like this, it will pay to inform the local coastguard where you are going, otherwise – and we have actually known it happen – your supposedly peaceful fishing might be interrupted by a full-scale cliff rescue team!

Normally, the fish that the shore angler will catch are the smaller specimens of almost all the various species that frequent our coastlines. But, watch out – for shore fishing is not without its surprises, and, at some time, you could find yourself hooked into something bigger and better than a lot of boat anglers would only dream of!

Supposedly 'deep water' fish will occasionally come well inshore, according to the vagaries of tide, weather and feeding availability, so, watch out for fireworks! In our view, this is probably the most interesting single factor about sea fishing – you never really know what's going to take your bait next. We know of an angler who was fishing the Blackwater estuary, in Essex – after tope, he was, with an enormous piece of herring on his hook.

What did he get? Would you believe a 4 lb (1.8 kg) fighting mullet? See what we mean? Highly unlikely, but nevertheless very possible.

Another chap was fishing for sole (delicious, grilled slowly and served with fresh lemon juice), and he was using tiny bits of ragworm on small hooks. Well, it's strange but true – this chap finished up with a socking great 32 lb (14.5 kg) conger eel – landed with much difficulty and skill, of course.

So, it all goes to prove that when you fish in the sea – shore or boat – you never really know what your next fish is going to be. Exciting, isn't it?

Don't get too carried away, though – the fish that the average shore angler is likely to bump into are pretty predictable, even according to the seasons. In summer, reckon on bass, mackerel, black bream and mullet. When winter comes, you'll probably find your cod, whiting, haddock, etc. Our advice is – gear up for the expected and tackle up accordingly, with size of hook and bait to suit the conditions. But, be ready at all times to modify your tackle and bait size for the unexpected.

When a good, heavy surf starts rolling on to the beach, the sport of surf-fishing can be enjoyed. This is only a natural extension of ordinary shore fishing, and it calls for longer casting techniques – also a firm, unshakable belief that the fish are feeding somewhere out in the pounding breakers. When you cast, go beyond the breaking waves into the area where the fish should be; don't cast too far, however, if the water inshore is deep and the breaking wave is 'short'. Attractive fish food will be collecting just behind the breakers, brought out by the backwash of the waves smashing on to the beach. The fish know this, particularly the bass – the classic quarry of the avid surf-caster. On sunny days, you may even see the bass, silhouetted in the roller itself, good proof that these fish actually enjoy the surf.

There's something basically simple about a man, a nice turbulent beach – and a good beach rod outfit; and a day spent this way will epitomize the very best in shore angling, in our view. And, on the way home in the car, he'll still be re-living, in his mind's eye, those great rollers pounding the shore, wondering at the beauty and power of it all – particularly if, carefully wrapped up in the boot, he has a bar of solid silvery scales – a bass, the 'Holy Grail' of the shore fisher.

Boat fishing

Having covered fishing from the shore, we now move on to boat fishing, which opens up a whole new world to the beginner. The British, by historical reputation, are a nation of seafarers, and modern men, whatever their particular calling may be, have a deeply rooted, latent love of the sea – and boats. A boat provides a man with a certain adventurous independence; in a boat, at sea, he can dissociate himself from mundane responsibilities of business and domestic pressures. The sea is, at one and the same time, a beautiful and tempestuous friend – and a dangerous enemy. When this newly found adventure is combined with the fascinating pursuit of hard-fighting fish, a firm and lasting bond is created between man, fish and sea; a wonderful and absorbing environment combined with a healthy and productive sport.

Having fished, extensively, from shores and boats, all over the world, we must confess to a certain bias towards boat fishing. Nothing is quite like it, but, and here we must inject a serious word of warning to the uninitiated, in comparison with shore fishing, the hazards and dangers of fishing from a boat are three-fold. Although the shore angler must keep a watchful eye on the encroaching tide at all times, and must be especially careful when fishing from high piers, jetties, etc., the boat angler has additional dangers with which to contend. However dangerous the seashore might be, it doesn't compare with the extra hazards of angling in a boat, offshore.

Weather at sea is extremely unpredictable; the fine, calm and sunny morning on the landing stage can so often turn into a cold, heavy squall, four miles offshore, with ten fathoms of icy, turbulent water waiting below. So, before you think about boat fishing, think more seriously about boats – and how to familiarize yourself with them. There are basically two types of fishing boats

– big and small, and, as a general guide, we suggest that, if you are a complete beginner, you start off in the largest possible boat. This is where the professional boatman comes in. All along our shores, in all the principal sea-fishing stations, you will find good, highly experienced boatmen, eager and willing to take you fishing. Put your trust in these men; they have spent a lifetime in their particular areas, learning by hard experience the vagaries of tide, current, wreck, hazard and depth.

So, please don't be tempted to rush off and buy a fragile little dinghy, then launch yourself off into the wide blue yonder. Get something a little bit more substantial under you – and opt for a good local boatman with a large seaworthy boat. As we have said, these chaps know what they're doing and where they're going, and we make no apologies for quoting this as being of secondary importance – they know where the fish are.

Think about it, logically. When you are fishing – beginning, that is – and you are unfamiliar with the moods and dangers of the open sea, the last thing you want to worry about is controlling and directing a boat. All this will be done for you, if you choose a competent boatman – in a safe, efficient boat. Which means, of course, that you can direct all your attention to fishing. Later on, when you have some experience – but only then – you might think about a smaller boat, or even a boat of your own.

Right, now for your first boat-fishing trip. Having booked your boat – or a place in a boat – for the express purpose of fishing, make sure that you have a good supply of bait. Most professional boatmen will do this for you, particularly if you make your needs known in advance. Rely on him. He will usually know which bait – or baits – the fish are 'taking' at that particular time, and, since he will be continually out at sea, fishing, will be able to provide good, really *fresh* baits like herring, slipper limpet, hermit crab, sprats, etc., all caught on the last tide. All lovely stuff! Make sure he brings plenty so that you won't run out of bait during a trip; he should know, anyway.

Now, let's get equipped for that first boat trip. Always take plenty of warm clothing, including a good waterproof coat, over-trousers and hat, for, even on a fine, warm summer's day at sea, you'll find that sea water from lines and reels, juice from the bait – and not forgetting the sudden, unexpected shower – will all find their way on to your clothing when you're sitting in a boat. As for food, well, that's up to the individual, but most 'boaters' will take two good-sized vacuum flasks, one containing hot soup, the other full of hot coffee, tea or whatever turns you on. Some boatmen will brew up scalding hot tea in big china mugs. Lovely!

Don't forget your tackle; everything prepared overnight, if possible, and every item checked and double-checked. Remember that if you get out to sea and you've forgotten some vital bit of equipment, like a reel, or something, you can't just walk back to the car to get it! We find that a standard 'check-list' of tackle is a good idea, and you can add extra items to this as required.

Add these to your list: a good waterproof cushion (long hours sitting in a boat can become uncomfortable); some of the inflatable cushions on the market are ideal, as they can be stowed away in a small space. A bag for (you hope!) putting your catch in, and, if you're inclined to suffer from *mal de mer* (seasickness, to you!) you should take the necessary precautions beforehand. A couple of good anti-seasick pills before you set out should do the trick; your friendly chemist will advise you. Still on the same subject, don't, for heaven's sake, indulge in a heavy, greasy fried breakfast before you go, particularly if you are new to boat fishing offshore. These last two precautions are for the good of the rest of the crew, as well as yourself, for nothing makes an angler feel more groggy (even an experienced one) than one of his companions hanging over the gunwale feeding the fish!

One particularly good travel pill we have discovered is called 'Dramamine', which will usually cure even the most persistently 'bad' sailor. Taken, as prescribed on the packet, about an hour before going afloat, it will normally combat *mal de mer* and give you a happy day on the high seas.

Right, we're ready to go, everything is stowed on board, the mooring lines are cast off and you're away. How far out you go will depend upon the boatman's idea of where the fish are; it could be ten miles offshore, or just a mile out. Anyway, the destination is reached, over goes the anchor and gradually the boat settles, riding easily to the anchor. On the way out, the other fishermen will have fixed their reels to the rod and threaded their lines through the rod-rings, and, following suit, like the ideal pupil you are, you will have done the same.

So, you've found your fishing 'mark', you're anchored and ready to fish. Now put a sliding boom on the line, stopped off with a bead, and a swivel tied to the end. Then tie on your trace – and ask the boatman for his advice on what size of hook to use; he will know what was caught successfully the day before, and will be able to judge, better than you, what hook to employ. Tie on your hook.

Now for a weight, and, here again, consult the boatman; he'll know how much weight will be required to 'hold bottom' successfully in the particular conditions of depth and tide, current, etc. Clip the weight to the boom. As for bait, this will vary according to the area and season, but, here again, rely upon the more experienced fishermen for advice. Put on the bait, perhaps a couple of big, lively worms, threaded carefully on to the hook. Your position in the boat will determine *how* you will fish. If you're positioned at the stern of the boat, then simply let the tide take the lead downtide, as you face aft (get used to these 'seafaring' terms!). If you are fishing at either side of the boat, then you'll be sitting facing 'outboard' with the line running out aft, downtide. For this reason, right-handed anglers are best positioned on the starboard (right) side, and the left-handers to port.

Let's assume that you have bagged the easiest fishing position, right aft; most reasonable boatmen, knowing that you're a complete beginner, will have put you there anyway. Lower your tackle over the side, giving out line steadily until, with a bonk! the lead touches bottom. Now raise the rod-top again and give a little more line, until you feel the lead bump the bottom again. In this way, you'll be able to 'use' the tide to work the lead away from the boat, into its fishing position. Keep repeating this process – lift rod point, give line – lift rod, give line, making sure that you are in continual contact with the lead. If you have chosen unwisely and your lead is too light, you'll see the line streaming downtide – without the lead contacting bottom. If it is too heavy, you'll find great difficulty in working the lead out, at all.

A word about lines for boat fishing. In very strong tides, or particularly deep water, the boat angler might find that, with orthodox lines, his tackle is weighted with about 2 lb (900 g) of lead and yet is still not firmly holding the bottom. In these circumstances, fishing becomes difficult, as bites are very hard to detect and, if small fish are hooked, there is little indication owing to the enormous weight of lead on the line.

This is where the wire fishing line comes in very handy. This type of line is usually made from multi-stranded stainless steel wire in a good range of breaking strains and one of its main advantages is its small diameter. For example, the boat angler fishing with a 1½ lb (680 g) lead on a 20 lb (9 kg) strain monofilament line can change to 20 lb (9 kg) wire line and find that he will only need a lead of 6 oz (170 g) to ½ lb (225 g). However, with these lines there are snags. Wire line is more difficult to handle than ordinary line, due to its tendency to springing and coiling. If you do use wire line, then we strongly advise you to employ a rod with 'roller' top and bottom rings or, better still, roller rings right through the rod. These rollers are designed to prevent wear and will allow the wire line to pass freely through the rings without kinking. This wire line can be hard on the hands, too, and when we use it, we usually wear a leather 'thumb stall' on the thumb that guides the line on to the reel.

The other big advantage to wire line, and which most anglers might find surprising the first time they use it, is the bite indication. This line is thin and has very little stretch, consequently it does not billow out downtide and the fast contact with the fish is quite dramatic – in fact, the first bite will be so positive, it will really surprise you. Even the smallest flatfish will register a bite that will be quite unmistakable, and if you contact a big fish, you'll think he's going to break the rod!

But, remember that because of the lack of stretch in this line, you must take special care when playing larger fish; if your clutch setting, on the reel, is too tight and the fish makes a sudden rush or plunge – twang – it's all over.

In deep water, there will be no need to work the lead gradually downtide, as its main purpose will be to get your bait, well down, away from the noise and disturbances in the boat. So, when fishing deep water, simply ensure your lead is on the bottom by lifting it off and feeling it 'bump' as it drops back. The most common fault with beginners is too light a lead – which is being forced, by the tide or current, off the bottom, so that it can't get the bait down to where it might do some good. Alternatively, the lead is too heavy, hitting bottom far too soon, with the angler giving out yards and yards of unnecessary line, which will 'balloon' out, downtide of the lead, with all that slack giving the illusion that the lead is riding off the bottom.

By continually lifting and 'bumping' your lead, you'll remain in constant contact with the tackle, which will be in a good fishing position – and not behaving like some underwater kite floating around in midwater. Bites from boats are usually quite determined and easy to detect, but there are days when the fish will bite more shyly, trying the angler's skill to the utmost. Usually though, your bite, when it comes, will be unmistakable, so, as in pier fishing, *never* leave your rod unattended or you might glance around, just in time to see it disappearing over the side!

Having got your bite, lift the rod – fairly gently – to tighten the line, culminating in a firm upward strike, then, according to all the rules, you should have a fish on. Whatever you do, don't, please, make unruly sideways 'slashes' when you strike; remember that you're in a boat with other people and space is restricted. Haphazard side-slashes could easily result in one crewman less. You could lose so many fishing friends that way!

Good, your fish is on and now you have to 'play' it. From a boat, this is normally fairly easy, but always remember that, if it's a big one, it has to be tired out before it comes inboard, and the best place to tire a fish is well down in the water, where the tide, depth and current are all against it; not on a long, difficult to manage line – or a too short line – and not on the surface, where anything can happen. Play your fish calmly and methodically; more fish have been lost through impatience than any other cause. All right, you're excited at what is probably your first boat-caught fish – and, judging by the interest of the crew members, it's a good one, and you're spoiling to see what it is you've got on. Don't be in a hurry, it's probably still full of fight and will be very difficult to handle; try to get it aboard before it's really played out and you'll probably be 'broken up' – and there's no glory in that.

When the fish is ready for the net or gaff, the boatman, if he's worth his salt, will be at your elbow ready to land it for you. Watch him carefully and you'll learn a lot. See how effortless he makes gaffing a fish appear. When you've really learned how, you can try it for yourself. The secret lies in a smooth upward lift – not a savage jerk.

You've got the fish in the boat. Good. Now give him the *coup de grâce*, with a heavy blunt instrument, as we described in the previous chapter; don't make a hash of it and don't let the poor thing die slowly; like all living creatures, fish have feelings.

After a while, when you really have captured the 'flavour' of boat fishing, you'll discover all this boat 'lore' for yourself. Most of these little unwritten rules and courtesies are designed, over many years, for the comfort and protection of everyone in the boat, so learn, digest and carry them out to the letter. In this way, you'll enjoy better sport and, what is probably more important, you'll be regarded, eventually, as someone worth having along when the next boat trip is planned.

Another of these little unwritten rules concerns the hooking of fish, by another crew member: if the chap next to you gets into a good fish, then you should reel in your own tackle at once. This makes good sense, for a fighting fish will, in all probability, wrap itself around other tackles in its fight to get away. Precautions like this will, in the long term, save time and prevent many unnecessary tangles.

All too soon, the day is at its end; fish have been caught – and lost – some good jokes have been told and shared and now it's time to get back to the shore; time to break down the tackle and stow your gear. If you have some good fish to your credit, your boatman might gut them for you, and, if you want to advance your sea-fishing knowledge even further, watch him carefully as he does it – it's quite an art and well worth knowing; follow his deft, professional movements, then, sometime, try it for yourself. Very soon, the greedy gulls will be following in your wake – knowing that there are rich pickings to be had as the fish 'offal' goes over the side.

So, for one day, you have been in the hands of a good professional boatman and, with luck, you've learned quite a lot. But, knowing you, you'll want to try it all out for yourself, perhaps with just one other experienced angler, in his boat. If you do, remember that you immediately take on much heavier responsibilities. You have to find the bait, between you. You have to decide whether it's safe to go afloat – in a much smaller boat. What's the weather like? Think carefully, before you decide. If you're in any doubt, wait a bit, see how the day develops – and if the forecast is bad, you have a very simple decision to make. Don't go!

Your day in the big boat, with a good crew and a highly experienced skipper, will prove to be almost entirely different to your exploits in a smaller boat, with just one companion. Apart from working the boat, anchoring it, gaffing and netting fish, perhaps even brewing the tea, you'll find it a busy and exciting day. Choose your boat – and its owner – very carefully. If he knows what he's about, he'll probably do all the navigating, provide charts, compass, flares and lifejackets; and, if he doesn't provide these things, as 'standard' equipment, don't go with him.

Fog, sudden bad weather, collisions, grounding – are all possible in a small boat in the open sea, so the omission of all, or any one of the aforementioned articles, could cost you your life.

Sorry to labour the point, but the sea is capricious, and you simply can't be too careful. Even if your small boat is equipped with the list of vital things we have already described, we strongly advise that you include, in your own kit, a lifejacket (preferably with light and whistle), a small pocket compass and a compact but efficient first-aid kit. If this sounds like carrying safety to extremes, remember that it will always serve as good 'back-up' equipment to whatever is in the boat. After all, things do get lost or misplaced.

This boat 'lore' really is of vital importance. For example, whether you go fishing in small or large boats, always obey the simple rules. Don't drop bait in the bilges – and don't cut it up on the polished and varnished mahogany of the vessel; you won't endear yourself to the owner. Most boat owners have a bait board for this purpose anyway. Be tidy. As it happens, both of the authors of this book are ex-naval men, and in early 'shipboard' days we thought the stringent discipline and fastidious tidiness afloat to be somewhat exaggerated, but we learned that it's all for a good purpose: neatness and cleanliness breeds greater efficiency. So, (another 'don't') don't make a big mess when gutting fish; a quick slosh with a mop and bucket doesn't always compensate. You'll find, by hard experience, that a good boat – and even more important – a good boatman, are hard to find; they're real treasures, so, having found them, act wisely and tidily; become a good sailor as well as a good angler. Do all this, and you'll be invited, with open arms, on that second trip.

Lately, more and more anglers are buying their own boats for fishing. Never has there been such a boom in boats and boating, and, knowing human nature, we are all too aware of the attractions of this type of 'pride of ownership'. But, we strongly advise you, before you venture into such rash independence, serve your 'apprenticeship' well. There is nothing more dangerous than a zealous but highly inexperienced angler afloat in a small, inadequate boat. In these circumstances, it is far better to put your trust in the professionals, they *know* when to venture out – or stay ashore. Have a quiet word with that august body, the Royal National Lifeboat Institution; they'll tell you, in no uncertain terms, that far the greater percentage of rescues at sea involve enthusiastic amateurs – not the experienced local boatmen, who, having read the signs, are beside their fires at home, waiting for the weather to moderate.

These Lifeboat men are to be much respected and admired, so, drop what you can afford into the Lifeboat collection box, but, to be fair to them – and their lives – don't take your little, uninitiated boat out in bad weather, or, even worse, ask a boat owner, whether professional or amateur, to take you out in his boat against his better judgement. Enjoy the sea and its bountiful fruits, but please don't court disaster.

Fish that the average boat angler will catch are many and varied, and, as in shore fishing, you should always tackle up according to the species you are after, having due regard to the time of year. Most of the fish already described in Chapter Two could turn up when you're fishing from a boat, plus, perhaps, the odd 'surprise' or two, for at sea the unexpected can happen.

In summertime, expect the usual bass, mullet, conger eels, etc., and, when fishing around wrecks, you're quite likely to meet up with a few cod, which will be 'left-overs' from the previous winter. Similarly, a cod angler will occasionally take a bass in the wintertime – and if he does, it will probably be a good one. Also, because the sea is such a rich and exciting treasure chest, the odd, semi-tropical fish will sometimes be caught by summer boat anglers; fish like the Ray's Bream which turns up, somewhere, every season – also the sunfish. If you should catch these, we suggest that you return them alive to the water. After all, they're really foreign 'tourists'.

Before we leave this section on boat fishing, let's talk about the method known as 'drifting'. This method is practised mostly in heavy tide conditions, over deep water and over wrecks and other 'rough' ground, and the boat, instead of being anchored, is allowed to drift at the speed of the tide or current. Fishing in this manner means that much lighter leads and finer tackle can be employed than for conventional 'anchored' boat fishing – with the pronounced effect that the fish, when he is hooked, puts up a much better fight, for, without the tide to fight against, he can use all his energies to combat the angler. There is a snag to this type of fishing, however, namely the continual stopping and starting of the boat's engine, and you'll find that a good proportion of time will be spent re-starting the motor and working back uptide to start a new 'drift'. We strongly suggest that if you fancy a good 'drifting' session, please do employ a good, experienced boatman, preferably one who knows the area well. Let him do all the work while you take care of the very pleasurable pursuit of drift-fishing. Remember that it would be dangerous for a novice to attempt all this; reading the special signs of the sea for potential hazards; rocks, wrecks and sandbanks, etc., just below the surface; the small coaster vessel looming up, suddenly through the mist – or the highly dangerous fog-bank, just when you least expect it. Other natural hazards include tidal races and overfalls, apart from sudden bad weather – which is a continual threat to the seafarer.

If you must drift, make sure that you know *where* you are drifting to, and always keep a weather eye cocked for possible trouble. Fishing is an extremely absorbing sport, and quite often, the angler is only really aware of the few square metres just around him. When he takes a 'break' after catching a fish, or to drink a hot cup of something, he might well find himself in some sort of weather or hazard trouble – without having realized it. So, if you're out drifting, watch the weather like a hawk, and if it worsens perceptibly, head well inshore and anchor the boat. If it gets worse still, then do what any prudent boatman would do when he's in doubt – get yourself, your crew and your boat back, as soon as possible, to a safe haven ashore, safe and dry.

Spinning, trolling, pirking and feathering

'Predatory' sea fish, that is, those that live on smaller fish, are often tempted by what we anglers call an 'artificial' bait, usually something made of metal; silvery, white or very shiny that flashes as it is drawn through the water. If you can contact these pre-dators, and all other conditions are right for this type of fishing, you'll find that they will attack your artificial lure with great gusto. Also, it is a very clean way of fishing, as no messy bait will be required.

One of the best examples of all is the mackerel – an extremely obliging predator who will continually strike at artificial lures, including 'spinners', 'feathers', 'jigs' or small 'pirks'. This sport-ing little mackerel will provide you with a very tasty meal – or bait for larger fish. Let's now clarify these artificial lures and get used to their names. A 'spinner' is what its title suggests; a small metal object, designed to spin as it is drawn through the water, and armed with hooks. In shape, it will usually resemble a small fish – and this is what the predator mistakes it for. Spinners are available in many different shapes and sizes, so be careful about becoming a 'collector', as they are very attractive, shiny things to have and most anglers have more than they need. The action of spinning tends to put an unwelcome kink in the line, so you should always employ an anti-kink lead, some 12–18 in (30–45 cm) in front of the spinner, which will be attached to the line by a spring-link swivel. The added weight of this lead will help your casting, too.

Another artificial lure which comes almost into the spinner category is the 'sandeel', usually made from rubber tubing over a large single hook, and the rubber is usually of a red, white or green colouring. In our own experience, the red or white seem to be the best attractors. An improved variety of the sandeel is the 'Red Gill', an imitation sandeel made from moulded rubber, again with a single hook at the business end, and which we regard as probably the best all-round artificial lure for salt water angling. 'Jigging' is really a method; you simply tie sandeels or spinners on short lengths of line, then attach the lot to the reel line. Complete the ensemble with an appropriate lead at the very end of the reel line, and you should have something like five or six smallish lures, spaced at short intervals along the line. To work the 'jig', lower it gently over the side of the pier – or boat – and give it a 'sink and draw' motion. This is done by sinking the tackle then pulling it up again with a firm upward pull on the rod. To repeat the process, lower the rod-tip again, until the lead sinks, then lift firmly upwards once more – and so on.

When you start, let your lead almost reach the bottom, then gradually work the tackle, in stages, up through the water until you find the 'strata' at which the fish are feeding. This is an excellent method of fishing for mackerel, pollack, coalfish, bass, cod and several other species, but, if you should suddenly encounter the larger fish, remember to increase the strength and weight of your tackle accordingly.

Pirking and feathering are similar to jigging. A pirk is a long, heavy, shiny piece of metal, with a large treble hook attached to one end, and will usually weigh from 3 oz (85 g) up to 26 oz (740 g). The pirk is a very good winter lure for cod, and in summer, will also account for good pollack and cod, particularly when fishing around sunken wrecks. They can be used on their own or in combination with jigs and feathers, and, as the pirk is such a heavy piece of equipment, no extra weight will be required on the line: simply attach it to the line with a spring-link swivel – and you're ready to fish.

Feathers are used in a similar way to jigs, and are probably the most popular of all the artificial sea-fishing lures. Summer mackerel fishing can be great fun, as you scan the surface for the first signs of your quarry. Watch for the seagulls first – and when they start to dive down to the water, screaming like mad and filling their beaks with small fish – you'll know that the whitebait, or 'brit', have arrived, being herded and harried upwards by the mackerel shoals below. Now, silently and carefully glide your boat close to the edge of the 'brit' shoals and drop over the 'feathers'. This tackle will consist of something like six feathered lures, complete with hooks, each on a short length of line attached to the main reel line, with a lead at the very end. Lower the tackle over the boat and you'll suddenly feel the lead stop in its journey to the bottom. At the same time, the whole tackle will jerk and shudder as the mackerel slash themselves on to the hooks, obviously mistaking the feathers for the teeming brit. Now reel in your catch – and you could find every hook has its mackerel, or other fish. When you find a good shoal, it will be easy to fill the bait box in no time at all – and you're still piling mackerel into the boat. Stop there, please, enough is enough, and senseless slaughter will not go well for you when you finally reach St Peter's Gate. No, when the box is full, put away the feathers and go after something bigger.

Feathers can, of course, be tied to larger hooks and will account for cod, pollack and coalfish too, mainly around wrecks or rocky ground. To tie feathers for cod, tie them on larger hooks than you would use for mackerel – and scale your tackle 'up' accordingly. Catch two or more decent-sized cod on a string of feathers and you'll soon see the sense of using stronger tackle; two big fish, on the same line, each fighting one against the other, would soon wreck the lighter mackerel feathers – and snap the lighter tackle.

'Trolling' is a somewhat specialized type of boat fishing, where a spinning lure or other artificial bait is literally towed behind a slow-moving boat. This method can account for lots of fish, as you can cover a lot of ground in a day. However, much heavier weights are needed than for other lure fishing, to keep the tackle at an efficient fishing level in the water. Also, this extra weight tends to spoil the fighting performance of all but the much larger fish. By far the best advantage of trolling is its ability to cover a lot of water – and to pinpoint where the fish are feeding. Once you have found them, and hooked a fish, stop the boat and fight it out; don't attempt to reel a fighting fish into a moving boat – if you value your tackle.

The general success of all artificial lure fishing relies upon one basic requirement – the fish must be able to *see* the lure. Consequently, you'll get the best results in clear water, with proportionately less chance as the water gets muddier or cloudier. That's why rocky coasts are generally better for this method, and why the river estuaries of the south-east coast of England rarely produce fish on feathers, pirk or jig – the fish simply can't see the lure through the muddy water. For the same reason, night fishing is rarely productive, but sometimes, in the last light of the day, or when a bright moon glows overhead, the mackerel can be taken, usually quite close to the surface. Alternatively, if your local pier or harbour wall is well lit, at night, you could fish the feathers, or other artificial lures, well on into the night.

Since visibility of lure is the keynote to good catches, always keep your spinners and pirks very clean and shiny, and always dry out your feathers – after washing them in fresh water.

There are other types of lure that do not catch fish, directly, but are employed as 'attractors' to lure the fish to your bait, and the best example is probably the 'flounder spoon', which is a smallish spoon lure of bright metal – or white plastic – tied to a 6 in (15 cm) length of nylon line, with a hook at the end. This hook is baited with worm or a strip of fish, and the complete thing fished at the end of a short flowing trace. In operation, it is simple and effective, as the spoon flutters and spins to catch the attention of feeding flounders and other fish. Up they come – to investigate the attractive, fluttering object and presto! – there's a nice juicy bit of worm or fish just behind it. What they don't know is that this tasty morsel conceals a hook! This method can work well for larger fish, like cod, and sometimes, when cod bites are few and far between, slip on one of these attractor spoons – and you could get a lot more bites. Try it sometime.

You can also fish a baited spoon on the 'paternoster' tackle, as described in the tackle chapter, and used over wrecks and rocky marks, it will often account for a good cod and pollack.

Always experiment with artificial lures, it will pay dividends. Vary the speed of retrieve, when fishing, or alternate the 'rhythm' of your jigging until you find the right one.

Unlike the rather 'lazy' method of simply dangling a baited tackle over the side of a boat, most types of lure fishing are somewhat strenuous, especially when working the larger pirks. An hour or two is very often enough for the average angler, as it can prove to be very tiring on the wrists and arms – not to mention the back. Not all lure fishing is like this, however, as a light spinner, cast across a calm inlet on a tranquil summer's evening, searching for the bass as they chase the sandeels over the sandy bottom, can be extremely delightful sport, with a flavour all its own.

We have a feeling you'll like artificial lure fishing. Learn your methods well, be sure to employ the right tackle, 'read' the water for signs of fish, and above all – at first, anyway – use a good boat with an equally good and experienced boatman. You'll love it.

Float fishing

Float fishing for sea fish can be an exciting, productive and very worthwhile method, although its application is limited to periods of relatively calm water.

Usually, an hour or so at top or bottom of the tide, when the water 'stands' for a while, is the best, also the boat angler will find float fishing while drifting quite profitable. Regardless of tides, however, there are occasions when any calm, sheltered water will prove suitable for float fishing; in harbours, docks or inlets protected from the main water movements, for example.

Mullet, bass, pollack, coalfish, mackerel, garfish, wrasse and black bream are the most commonly caught fish when using a float, and, after you have 'cut your teeth' on the smaller fish and graduated to shark fishing, you'll find a heavy form of float tackle is often employed, but let's leave that, for now. For float fishing, a special terminal (and) tackle is needed, as this is very important for success. Most of the floats sold for sea fishing are far too large; you have probably seen them – great, highly coloured cigar-shaped things about 12 in (30 cm) long. Avoid these, and go for something quite a bit smaller; the larger types of freshwater fishing floats are ideal.

For mullet fishing, we use an even smaller float, similar to the ones used for freshwater canal fishing, as these fish – in spite of their great strength at the end of a line – are shy and sensitive biters. Such a float, together with a small hook and a couple of small shot on the line, can be cast between boats moored in a harbour or river estuary and will provide splendid sport – but you must get the bait right. Baits for mullet fishing are many and varied, and include bread, small worms, bits of fish, maggots, strands of water weed, bacon fat, banana, cheese paste, etc. The list is almost endless. But we have two special favourites. One is simply white bread – but employed in a rather special way. Here's how. Mix up about half a bucketful of well wetted and mashed bread, then blend in, thoroughly, about two ounces (50 grams) of pilchard oil (get it from your bait shop or tackle dealer). Then place the mixture in a fine-meshed vegetable sack and, if you're fishing in a harbour or estuary, hang the bag in your chosen swim. Every so often, jerk the bag to release particles of oily mush and, pretty soon, you'll get the mullet interested. Don't be in too much of a hurry though, it could take several days of baiting-up at high tide before you really get the mullet on the feed.

When you have them going, put a small piece of soft bread-

paste on the hook (remembering to anoint it with a little pilchard oil) and you should start to get bites. These bites will vary
between timid little tweaks and violent plunging stabs. Mullet
fight well and hard and, on light tackle such as we have described,
will give you great sport. Now for the second method. On open
beaches during hot summers, you'll sometimes find, after the
spring gales, rafts of seaweed washed ashore above high-water
mark – and they will usually be very smelly and buzzing with flies.
When you find one, take a garden fork – and a deep breath – and
turn over the rotting weed. Your 'treasure' lies underneath –
masses of sand-hoppers and other beach insects and some nasty
looking white maggots. These you will use for bait.

Then, thread on to your line a small round cork float (we call
it a 'pilot' float) which is about ¾ in (20 mm) in diameter. Now,
about 18 in (45 cm) up the line, fix on a smaller piece of cork or
quill using two float-caps, one at each end. This is your indicator
proper. Then tie on a small hook, about size 12 or 14 and bait
this with maggots, either one fat one or a couple of smaller ones,
being very careful to hook them through the skin at the 'blunt'
end, to prevent them from bursting. Having decided which part
of the water you're going to fish, you'll need some 'round bait' –
and, although you might think it ridiculous, this will be your rotting seaweed, pitched into your swim by the forkful. Remember,
this muck is literally crawling with insects and maggots and, with
luck, you should have the mullet going in no time. Swing out
your baited tackle, with the larger float acting as a 'marker' and
the smaller float as the indicator. Watch the tiny float like a
hawk, and, as soon as it dips – strike!

As you would guess, this method is specially suited to calm
summer evenings – but believe us, it does produce fish. Occasionally, a bass or pollack will join in the fun – then watch out for
fireworks!

The more traditional float fishing, for fish like mackerel, garfish, bass, pollack, etc., is a little different and for this we will use a
'sliding' float. This float has a hollow tube right through the
centre, through which the line passes. To fix up this tackle, the
sliding float is first threaded on to the line, then a weight, usually

a spiral or barrel lead, is added, is just sufficient to 'cock' the float and make it stand upright in the water. When a suitable hook has been tied on, the tackle is ready – but for one very important item, the 'stop' knot that will determine the depth at which the tackle will fish. When this tackle is cast into the water, the lead will pull the line through the float until the weight hits the bottom, leaving the float lying on the surface. The purpose of the 'stop' knot is to jam against the top of the float to prevent any more line sliding through. By adjusting the distance of the knot from the hook, the fishing depth can be controlled.

Mackerel, for example, are usually caught in shallow coastal waters some 6 ft (1.8 m) to 10 ft (3 m) under the surface. So, when you start fishing for them, you begin at about 6 ft (1.8 m) and increase the depth, as required, until you locate the feeding fish. This special – and very useful – stop knot can be found among the other knot illustrations in this book.

Baits for float fishing are many and varied, but, in our own experience, the natural baits like prawns, small fish, squid and fish strips and worms seem to take the better fish. As for the rest of your tackle, always use as fine a line as possible, to give your float rig delicacy and living movement. A long, fine rod will be an asset, too.

Striking can be a difficult art when float fishing in the sea. Most bites will register as a quick 'bob' or two on the float, followed by a straight plunge under. No problem with these bites – simply strike as the float disappears. Other bites, depending upon the water conditions at the time, could be less decisive, it's up to you; watch the float, never let it out of your sight – and you'll catch fish. One golden rule. Always keep a 'tidy' line between float and rod-tip, no slack curves or snaky lines, please. Remember, when you strike, any slack line must be taken up – quickly – or the fish will be lost.

Yes, float fishing has its advantages – and its drawbacks, if not used in proper context. One thing is for sure, though. As far as presentation is concerned, it is the most natural fishing method available.

6 Safety for the sea angler

Every year, thousands of people take up sea fishing for the first time. Most of them come from inland, and, apart from an occasional row around the park lake on Sunday afternoon, they know nothing of the water, its uncertainty and, in particular, the very real dangers of putting to sea in a small boat.

Regularly, the newspapers tell of large ocean-going vessels, of all types, foundering or actually sinking, through adverse weather conditions. Think about it. Then decide what chance your own little 'cockle shell' would stand if a really heavy squall or storm broke suddenly, six miles offshore.

So, to help you keep life and limb intact, here's a simple check-list for beginners to boat fishing in the sea.

Make sure your boat is of a suitable and adequate size for the number of anglers it will be carrying. *Make sure* it is properly equipped with:

oars, bailer, at least one anchor and warp, compass, bucket, row-locks (tied to thwarts), flares, spare fuel, whistle for foggy weather, charts, first-aid kit and a sturdy waterproof torch (make sure the batteries are in good order); in addition, each separate angler should have his own lifejacket (make sure it is a good fit), waterproof, warm clothing, hot drink and food.

Before you put to sea, *make sure* the weather forecast service is consulted. If the forecast is bad, or very uncertain, *make sure* you stay ashore. If in doubt, get advice from the local boatmen, fishermen or harbour staff; they will know local conditions and will be aware of all the tell-tale weather signs. Rely on them. Remember that they are probably also members of the Local Life-boat service – so if you get into trouble *they* will have to come to your rescue.

Make sure that someone knows where you are going. Give your time of departure and estimated time of return, preferably to the local coastguard, at the same time indicating roughly where you will be fishing.

Make sure you don't take raw beginners out to sea on really rough days – you could put them off sea fishing for life! *Make sure* that your fishing tackle is tidy and neatly stowed in the boat, so that you – or your companions – won't trip over it. *Make sure* that your boat is always kept in a clean and neat condition. Tidiness spells efficiency – the more efficient you are, the fewer accidents you will have.

Make sure that the boat plug is in *before* you launch. *Make sure* bait is not left to fall on the bottom boards of the boat; it will make the going slippery – and dangerous. Most boat skippers (and if you get a boat, that will include *you*) are proud of their vessels – so if you're cutting up bait, use a good, solid bait board – not the woodwork of the boat!

Make sure you get to Heaven when you die – if you catch fish, kill them very quickly with a smart rap on the skull with a row-lock, heavy pliers, or similarly heavy object; cut out suffering, fish have feelings. And, back to tidiness again, always keep your fish in a neat plastic container.

Always include a bucket in your equipment; it can be used as a 'sea anchor' on the end of a rope, and will help to steady the boat at sea, if the engine fails. It's also very handy for gutting fish, washing down, etc., and can even make a makeshift toilet or a useful receptacle for someone who is overcome by sea sickness.

Don't be afraid to take sea sickness pills before putting to sea; there's nothing 'cissy' about taking precautions. Anyway, it's far better than having a good day's fishing ruined by being continually sick. If you, or someone else is seasick in a boat, lie down if possible and get ashore as soon as you can.

Keep your weather eye open – all the time. Remember that the tide against the wind will make the seas choppy and confused. On a bad day with wind and tide together, remember that it will get worse when the tide changes. Whatever you do, don't take chances in boats: mistakes can cost you your boat, or even worse, your life.

Beach, pier and rock fishing

Don't take chances of being washed into the sea by a sudden and unexpected large wave. During the week that this chapter was written, two sea anglers were drowned, when they were knocked from their rock-fishing positions by a freak wave. Remember that, as the tide rises to the shore, the height of the waves will usually increase, so stand well back if you are rock fishing. If the weather turns rough, don't go out on the jetty, or if you are beach fishing, move higher up the beach. At most resorts, the piers are closed to anglers during rough weather, but don't rely on this; get off the pier if things start getting rough.

Watch out for flying leads, hooks and tackles. Casting is by far the biggest single danger to anglers and spectators alike. *Always* cast overhead style only in crowded places; never a side swing. Even then, only start to cast when it's clear around you and you've announced the fact that you're going to cast in a loud voice.

Don't push your way onto a crowded pier or jetty and spoil the sport of others. *Ask* if you can join in and if invited, always leave a reasonable amount of space between you and those anglers at either side. *Don't* leave old bait, newspapers, wrappers, beer cans or any other rubbish lying around. Any bait left unused when you leave can be given to other anglers – who might be very glad to get it. Failing this, throw it into the sea. Any fish heads or guts should also be thrown into the sea – where sea birds will quickly dispose of them. *Always* take 'non-organic' garbage, like plastic film and bottles, and metal containers of all kinds, home with you and dispose of them with the refuse collector. *Always* be very careful with glass bottles; they're lethal if left on a beach, as even if intact when discarded, the very next spell of rough weather will smash them – causing great danger to children and bathers.

General safety points

Distress and drowning: if you see anyone in distress in the water, help them, if you can, right away. If you cannot, summon help quickly by calling the local police or coastguard (for either, simply dial 999 on the telephone). If you saw a distress flare, try to give the exact time, distance and bearing, if possible. Learn how to apply mouth-to-mouth resuscitation ('kiss of life'). You will probably never need to use it, but it's an extremely useful thing to know, at sea or inland. If you discover someone in the water, get him into the boat by pulling him over the stern – never over the side, or the boat could capsize. People rescued in this way should be kept as warm as possible and provided with a hot drink, if they are able to drink. Unconscious victims should have their breathing checked frequently, and if breathing has stopped, then apply mouth-to-mouth resuscitation immediately, continuing this until he revives or professional help arrives. Don't give up, and if fellow rescuers are with you, take the revival attempts in turns to avoid fatigue.

Care of tackle

Salt water is particularly hard on tackle, and will quickly cause corrosion to unprotected parts. It will also permeate other tackle, so follow these hints closely – and save money on your tackle.

Don't leave wet, salty tackle in the tackle-bag until the next trip. Dry and clean everything as soon as possible when you arrive home and, if necessary, apply oil to reels and other tackle with moving parts needing lubrication. Waterproof clothing won't last for ever, particularly if it is left, wet, in a heap somewhere. *Always* hang it up to air, after use, preferably in a fairly warm dry room. *Always* check fishing line after each outing. Look for bad splits, cuts or abrasions that could cost you a good fish next time out. If in doubt, always cut off a few yards from the end of the line – that's where the wear occurs.

Always protect hooks from rust. Only take a limited number out with you when you go fishing, then, if your hook box gets a dousing, you haven't spoiled the lot. *Do not* take fishing reels to pieces unless you really thoroughly understand the mechanism. Modern reels are very sophisticated pieces of machinery. If in doubt, take them back to your tackle dealer or return them to the manufacturer for repair. *Never* leave loose hooks or lures lying around at home (or anywhere else) for obvious reasons. To see a small child having a hook cut out of its hand by a doctor is a heartbreaking sight. *Neatness* breeds efficiency. Get into the professional seafarer's way of keeping everything 'ship-shape'. Be tidy, keep safe and enjoy your fishing.

7 A day's sea fishing with Arthur and Alan

Young Philip has been fishing – for coarse fish – for about two years now, but was dying to try his hand at sea fishing. So, that evening, after having arranged a fishing trip for the three of us on the south-east coast, I brought Phil over to Alan's fishing den for a bit of preliminary instruction.

Alan was busy sorting out the tackle when we arrived. 'Hello Phil, ready for your first sea trip tomorrow? Good lad, I think you'll enjoy it, if the weather stays right. Now, have a look at this light, hollow-glass boat rod – this is what you'll be using, so get the feel of it, now. Here's your reel, it's a multiplier, with a strong metal spool, and I've filled it with plenty of good 20 lb [900 kg] breaking strain line. Yes, I know it's all a bit different to freshwater tackle, but it's quite easy, once you get the hang of it. Look, put the rod together and slot the reel into its fitting and tighten it up. That's it, fine. Now, look at the reel. This is the slipping clutch control, this "star" behind the handle, and this little lever on the same side is the "free spool" lever; show Phil how they work, Arthur, I'm going to sort out a few more bits of tackle from my bag.'

While I ran through the reel controls with Phil, Alan came back with a small box containing some swivels, plain and link spring types, some Clement and Kilmore booms, a good variety of hooks, a few beads and a small but sharp sheath knife. He also had a canvas bag holding a selection of leads, weighing from 3 oz (85 g) to 1½ lb (680 g). Over his arm was an elderly – but serviceable – waterproof coat and a new lifejacket. 'These are for you Phil, and I suggest that you wear a good woollen sweater or two tomorrow, with this jacket on top, to keep the wind and weather out, and, most important of all, here's a lifejacket, which I'm sure my wife Joy won't mind you borrowing for a while. The boatman will almost certainly have one, but in case he hasn't one your size, take this one along. Now, my tackle's all ready in the garage, and if I know Arthur, he's stowed his neatly in his car – oh, I almost forgot, did you bring the squid and herring bait from your deep freeze? You did – good man, I'll pop them in my freezer overnight and let them thaw out on the way to the coast tomorrow.'

I brought the squid and herring in. 'Hey Al, did the bait arrive today?' A satisfied smile spread across Alan's face. 'Yes mate – I've got some really lovely lugworms – and some great king rag too! Old Robbie, my Norfolk bait digger, sent the lug down on the train, and Joe, the Southend digger, brought the ragworm up to me on Friday afternoon. Well, he was coming up this way anyway, and dropped them in. I'm glad he did! They're lying on the cold end of the garage floor, which reminds me, I'd better have a look at them and change the paper under the lugworm. The ragworm will need re-wrapping by now, too.'

Phil, keen as mustard, was sorting through the tackle and I gave him some good advice. 'Notice how Al's got the bait situation sewn up, Phil. It's most important to have really good, reliable bait diggers – and look after them; bait's an essential part of all sea fishing, as you'll discover.'

Alan came back with a flat wooden box with a handle, and lined with newspaper. As he peeled off the top covering, a black and brown mass of lugworm was revealed. 'Great,' I said. 'What's the ragworm like?'

'Just as good,' commented Alan, as he went out and returned with a small cardboard box filled with small rolls of newspaper, which, when unfolded, brought to light the first red-green, multi-legged ragworm. Phil was really intrigued. 'Watch out for these babies, Phil, they actually bite,' commented Alan. 'They have a recessed mouth, with a tiny parrot-like beak – and if you don't watch out, they'll give you quite a nip – the big ones can actually draw blood. So, if you don't want to get bitten, handle them firmly and quickly, then they won't get the chance. Tell you what, give Arthur a hand to change the wrapping, it helps keep the worms nice and fresh – which is of vital importance. You do that, and I'll ring Peter, our boatman for tomorrow. I'll also check with the local coastguard to see what the weather's going to be like in that area tomorrow.'

Al went across to the desk, and soon he was through to the Essex coast. 'Hello, Peter? Alan Vare here. How's things? Are we all right for tomorrow? Good, what's being caught at the moment? Well, that sounds like a good mixed bag. Plenty of mackerel, bream, flatfish, thornback rays, what was that? Small tope – and the odd pollack and cod from the wrecks. Great, sounds great. I'll bring some pirks and sandeels along, could be useful. Do what? Conger eels? Well, if we can get over that new wreck of yours tomorrow, at slack water, we should contact a conger or two. Yes, I'll make sure we have a heavy rod and some tough wire traces for the job. What's the forecast? North-westerly wind, force two to three, great, it couldn't be much better. Right Peter, see you at the usual place, about 8.30. Goodnight, mate.'

'Well, mates,' said Alan, 'that's all sorted out, we're picking up Peter at about 8.30 tomorrow morning, so off you go Phil, we'll call for you at 6.15 a.m. We've a long way to go – so mind you're awake and ready to move out.'

The following morning, Alan was awake by 5 a.m. and, knowing that further sleep would be impossible, turned off the alarm clock and crept downstairs, to fill vacuum flasks and sort out the day's food from the fridge. By 6 a.m. he'd packed the final items into the estate car and checked the welfare of his beloved bait. By 7.30 Alan, myself and Phil were peering, hopefully, over the harbour wall at the boat, a modern glass-fibre 'Fast Fisherman' craft, one of the new breed of boats built specifically with anglers in mind. Alan looked carefully around the deserted harbour. 'No sign of Peter, the lazy blighter,' he said. 'Let's go and get some breakfast.'

The little harbourside café was full of heavily sweatered seamen, fishermen, charter boat skippers and the odd dockworker, and Philip's eyes were wide with the wonder and anticipation of of it all. Soon, their skipper, Peter, turned up, and all the gear and bait lowered into the *Starfisher*, waiting at the quayside. The moorings were cast off and the boat made its way slowly out of the harbour. 'The mackerel were quite close in, yesterday,' remarked Peter. 'Tackle up with feathers and we'll catch some for bait.'

The boat stopped just outside the harbour wall, and everyone got their feather tackle together. Alan was helping Philip to tackle up, and soon they were both lowering the leaded tackles over the side. 'They're here,' I said quietly, and the others looked at my jerking rod-tip, as the mackerel on my hooks struggled to free themselves. Then, reeling in smoothly, I swung four lovely mackerel aboard, unhooking them swiftly and giving each one a quick whack with the 'priest', before dropping them into the waiting bait tub.

Soon, Philip and Alan were into the mackerel, too, and in no time there were eighteen shimmering mackerel in the box. 'Right,' said Peter, in a businesslike voice. 'Let's go fishing.' And, pulling back the throttles, he surged the boat forward to the open sea.

Half an hour later and some eight miles from the shore, the anchor was dropped over the side. Philip and I tackled up with flowing traces and medium-sized hooks, only one hook to a trace. I helped Phil to put the final touches to his tackle, and advised him to put some ragworm on his hooks. Peter, the skipper, was peering intently into his echo-sounder. 'We're over sand here,' he said 'Pretty close to a rock patch; I'll just make sure the boat has settled to the anchor rope. Right, that's it. Now, lower your tackle out – slowly, Phil – what's your lead? 8 oz [227 g]. That's about right, it should allow you to get the tackle downtide a bit.'

As Phil's lead bumped the bottom, he allowed the tide to pull some line off the reel, and, with some instruction from Alan, the tackle was worked, up and down, with the tide, away from the boat. I followed suit, taking care not to get my tackle too close to Phil's. Alan, meantime, had set up a heavier rod, and was now busy threading a side of a mackerel on to a large hook, which was mounted on a length of fine nylon-covered wire. 'I'm going after the tope,' he declared. 'Look Phil, I've got a slightly sturdier rod, some 20 lb [9 kg] monofilament line and a tough wire trace.'

At the same time, Peter, who was just as keen on tope fishing as Alan, was attaching a mackerel side to similar tackle. Soon, all four tackles were out, and not a word was spoken, everyone was concentrating for that first bite of the day. Then Phil's rod-top quivered and dipped. 'Strike!' shouted the other three, almost as one voice, and setting his teeth, Phil struck. The rod arched over and jerked violently, and, after some advice from his three companions, he had a small thornback ray in the bottom of the boat, competently netted by Peter. 'Well done, Phil,' said Peter. 'She's only about 8 lb [3.5 kg] but for a first fish that's a jolly good start!'

Soon afterwards, Peter's own reel ratchet screamed its warning, and, picking up the rod, he allowed the line to run off the reel, as the fish rushed away from the boat. 'Looks like a tope, Pete,' said Alan, and Peter nodded, his eyes still intently watching the line running smoothly from the reel, silently now, as he had slipped off the ratchet. Suddenly, the 'run' stopped – as quickly as it had begun, and Phil, thinking that the fish had become de-tached, watched each face in turn, waiting for the disappointed remarks. None came. All three were watching the line with rapt attention. Off the line went, again, and with a smooth upward sweep of the rod, Peter set the hook into the running fish.

A fierce battle between man and fish followed, run after run being stopped and line retrieved, until, at last, Alan's long arm reached over the boat's side and he 'tailed' the tope into the boat. Peter got his long-handled pliers working to remove the hook, while Alan and I held the fish down with pieces of sacking. Phil was intrigued. 'Gosh, that's a beauty!' he said, in an awed voice. 'Not bad,' replied Alan, 'but you've got to watch the teeth, Phil. They're really razor-sharp.' Then he carefully lifted the tope over the side and released it. The fish, after resting in the tide for a while, swam slowly downwards into the water and disappeared from view. 'Time for tea!' shouted Peter – and nobody argued.

And so the day continued. I caught a good dogfish and several bream, and Phil was amazed how hard the little bream fought on such strong tackle. Then Phil caught a couple of nice bream him-self, and, a little later, boated a good plaice of about 3 lb (1.4 kg). Peter, persevering with his tope tackle, had another run, but the fish dropped the bait after a couple of rushes. Alan had one dog-fish, and, just as everyone was preparing to pack up, a fish that didn't put up much of a fight – and turned out to be a small turbot of 7 lb (3 kg). On the way back, the weather was still beautifully mild and calm, so Peter let Philip steer the *Starfish* most of the way in, watched by Alan's expert eye, while he gutted the fish, skinned the dogfish and cut up the thornback ray.

Regretfully, we said goodbye to Peter, with a firm promise that we'd be back again, soon. Phil seemed particularly loath to leave, declaring that, if this was sea angling – it was for him! When everything, including the fish, was stowed in the car, we headed for home, tired but happy, and excited chatter punctuated the journey. Then it was our respective homes, early to bed – and the deep, untroubled sleep of the happy sportsman.

Index

Colin Willock
The ABC of Fishing £1.95

'Excellent... A comprehensive guide to angling for coarse, sea and game fish in British waters' EVENING NEWS

'Edited by one of the foremost angling authors of the present day, this book will surely take its place among the classics of angling literature' ANGLER'S WORLD

Fred Buller
Pike £1.95

'Fred Buller deals with methods, practice, weather, tackle, all the practical things a would-be pike fisherman needs to know... copiously illustrated, well and clearly written' TROUT & SALMON

edited by Kenneth Mansfield
Coarse Fishing 70p

Seven authors, each well known for their writing on angling topics, provide the complete handbook on coarse fishing for every angler. All the main species are dealt with individually, together with full descriptions of tackle and techniques. Baits – how to find, clean and use them – are covered in the same comprehensive manner, and there is a wealth of other useful information.